To Celeste
with best regards

Lou Frieman

"SHRINK"

"This book is about a spirit of love for what is alive,
be it people, animals, nature; a love for creation of
which we are part. It is about caring for patients, aiming at intimate communications free of judgments and
directives, and establishing creative therapeutic communities. This motivating spirit is apparent throughout
this modest autobiography. Our psychiatric profession
has lost spirit and heart. Fierman shows us that with
loving care and creative imagination we can revitalize
our work and our lives."

—Marianne Horney Eckardt, M.D.,
former president of the American Academy
of Psychoanalysis and Dynamic Psychiatry

Also by Louis B. Fierman, M.D.

Effective Psychotherapy:
The Contribution of Hellmuth Kaiser
(Edited by Louis B. Fierman, M.D.)

The Therapist Is the Therapy:
Effective Psychotherapy II

Freeing the Human Spirit:
A Psychiatrist's Journal

"SHRINK"

On Becoming
a Psychotherapist

LOUIS B. FIERMAN, M.D.

Blue Dolphin

Copyright © 2006 Louis B. Fierman

Published by Blue Dolphin Publishing, Inc.
P.O. Box 8, Nevada City, CA 95959
Orders: 1-800-643-0765
Web: www.bluedolphinpublishing.com

ISBN: 1-57733-183-4

Library of Congress Cataloging-in-Publication Data

Fierman, Louis B.
  "Shrink" : on becoming a psychotherapist / Louis B. Fierman.
      p. ; cm.
  Includes bibliographical references and index.
  ISBN 1-57733-183-4 (hardcover : alk. paper)
  1. Psychotherapy—Anecdotes. 2. Psychotherapist and
  patient—Anecdotes. 3. Psychology—Study and teaching—
  Anecdotes. I. Title.
  [DNLM: 1. Fierman, Louis B. 2. Psychiatry—Personal
  Narratives. 3. Psychotherapy—Personal Narratives.
  WZ 100 F465 2006]

  RC480.5.F54 2006
  616.890092—dc22
  [B]
                                          2006017163

Printed in the United States of America

10   9   8   7   6   5   4   3   2   1

To Dan and Laurie

CONTENTS

ACKNOWLEDGMENTS

It has been my good fortune while writing this book to receive much encouragement, support and feedback from my wife, Ella Yensen, Ph.D., who has been a major influence on my values, beliefs, character and behavior ever since we first met and fell in love in college in 1940. Her insights and philosophy pervade the book's entire manuscript, especially the *Epilogue*.

Also very helpful were my conversations about the book with my son, Dan; my son-in-law, Daryll Kale; my friends Howard P. Kahn, Ph.D.; Dorothy Karg; Sey Nishimura, Ph.D.; John M. Rakusin, Ph.D.; and his wife, Kim; my niece, Cherie Reminick; my nephew, Howard Reminick, Ph.D.; and his wife, Lee; Alan P. Towbin, Ph.D.; and his wife, Linda; and my publisher, Paul M. Clemens.

I am especially thankful to my daughter, Lauren, and to Virginia Abbot Shia Lovig, for their expert critique of the quality of the writing throughout the manuscript.

PREFACE

This book of autobiographical recollections describes events that moved me along a path to becoming a psychotherapist, and experiences that eventually proved useful in my conduct as a therapist. Central to the concept is the fact that until I was a sophomore in college I had never given the slightest consideration to pursuing a medical career, let alone becoming a psychiatrist psychotherapist. Yet seemingly disparate and unrelated parts of my life came together at age twenty to form an ambition and determination to become just that.

The background of the book is my life itself: born into a poor immigrant family, raised in a "melting pot" bustling community, attending crowded public schools, winning a competitive scholarship to college, persuaded by my brother, Frank, to major in pre-med rather than chemistry, accepted by a medical school, tuition paid by a philanthropist, serving in the United States Army Medical

Corps during WWII, followed by residencies in internal
medicine and psychiatry at Yale; three years of personal
psychotherapy, learning a dynamic, humanistic, interpersonal approach to psychotherapy from my therapist,
Hellmuth Kaiser, and, finally emerging as a therapist.

1

BEGINNINGS

1

BEGINNINGS

"Pa, how'd you get that scar on your forehead?"

My father, Benjamin Fierman, was a robust, cheerful, pot-bellied man, seated at his sewing machine in his tailor shop, repairing a customer's trousers while smoking one of the cigarettes that he carefully made each evening, sprinkling a row of powdered tobacco onto a thin small sheet of cigarette paper, then rolling it and licking the edge to produce a smokable cigarette. "Well, Lazeral," he replied (Lazeral was my Yiddish family nickname, derived from the Hebrew Biblical name, Eleazar,) "I've told you already that I joined the Menshevic Party in Odessa when I was about eighteen." He went on to describe his participation in an abortive Menshevic revolution in Russia that failed but was followed later by a successful Communist overthrow of the Czar's government. "We threw cobblestones from the street at government buildings and we tried to shut them down by blocking the streets. We would

stand in a row and lock our arms together to block the
street. One day the Cossacks arrived on their horses and
they charged us, swinging their sabers at us as we tried to
run away. One of them hit my head and cut my forehead,
but I was able to get away, and that's what gave me that
scar."

That conversation with my father took place when I
was about ten and he about forty-four. It was unusual for
us to talk about his past since as a child and teenager I had
little interest in my parents' lives in Europe, and they had
little interest in talking about it. But over the years I did
learn bit by bit about their histories and how they had
emigrated as refugees, my mother, Rebecca Ghidaleson,
from Bucharest, Rumania, and my father, from Bessarabia, Russia.

He had completed public school in Bessarabia, ap-
prenticed himself to a local tailor and learned his trade.
Only after I reached adulthood did I learn that he had
been married before in Russia and had two children. At
age twenty-four he decided in 1912 to emigrate to
America with his family to avoid being drafted into the
Czar's army which was preparing for war with Germany
and was notorious for its anti-Semitic abuse of its own
Jewish soldiers.

Jewish immigrants like my mother and father were
welcomed and supported by Jewish communities in
America. On arrival in New York they would be provided
with food, shelter and time to search for a mate and a job.
If unsuccessful, they would move on to another city until
they found a compatible spouse and suitable employment.
Those who landed at Ellis Island would begin their search
in Harlem and then move on to Newark, Philadelphia,
Pittsburgh, Youngstown, Cleveland, Toledo and finally
Detroit. I recall as a child that strange men would fre-

quently arrive and stay at our small apartment for several days, sleeping nights on the couch, chairs or floor, and then most would gradually disappear. A few would settle down and live nearby and visit my parents from time-to-time. When some of the young ones would call my mother "Mother," I assumed we were related, but learned later from my mother that they were all immigrants who had been sheltered by my parents and who had found a job and a spouse in Cleveland and had not moved on as did the others.

My mother told me that she had been raised on her father's farm near Bucharest, Rumania. She and her three sisters were all denied schooling by the tyrannical Rumanian government. When she was seventeen, her father died and she emigrated with her mother, sisters and young brother to seek their fortunes in "wonderland America." In the U.S.A. they made their way to Cleveland, Ohio, where she found employment in a cigar factory. I marveled at my parents' courage to leave their hostile native lands and travel as refugees with very limited resources to lead a new life in a distant foreign land.

My father and his family also settled in Cleveland, Ohio, where he found employment in a clothing factory. His wife became ill after an attempted abortion and she died in Cleveland. He placed his five-year-old daughter and three-year-old son in an orphanage while he searched for a spouse to replace their dead mother. A Jewish matchmaker referred him to my mother.

She was a beautiful, lively, intelligent though illiterate, twenty-year-old, strong-willed, devout Jewish woman. She told me how my father courted her. For his first encounter my dad waited with flowers outside the factory door for her to appear at the end of her day's work. She recalled, "He was honest about his looking for a replacement mother for his children and I liked him for that, but I wasn't at all interested in his proposal." Not one to accept "No" for an answer, my father then retrieved his children from the orphanage and with them waited again the next day at the factory door for Rebecca to emerge. She told me, "When I saw those two adorable children, I could not resist and I agreed to consider his proposal that we marry and for me to raise them as my own." After a few weeks of courtship, they married. As I observed and experienced their relationship over the years, it was clear to me that they enjoyed a deep mutual love and commitment to each other that went far beyond the original negotiations that led to their marriage.

They settled in a rental apartment on Kinsman Road in east-side Cleveland, a lower middle-class neighborhood teeming with Jews, Catholics, Protestants, Hispanics, Blacks, Irish, Poles, Russians and Italians, a proverbial "American Melting Pot." Mother taught herself to speak English, read phonetically and use the city's trolley street cars to travel about the city. Cleveland then had an excellent low cost, mass-transit system of trolley street cars for its one-million-plus pedestrians. Unfortunately, in later years, a cabal of bus manufacturers, gasoline corporations and rubber tire companies conspired to politically influence Cleveland and other similar cities to replace their efficient trolley systems with high cost systems of gasoline guzzling, pollution exhausting, noisy motor buses.

My parents were energetic, enterprising and determined to survive in their new, bustling American land of opportunity. Their overriding selfless goal was to provide a secure, happy home for their children, free from the pogroms and religious persecutions of their native lands. While both were observant Jews, only my mother was

deeply devout. My father and siblings respectfully indulged my mother's compliance with the many rituals and
details of orthodox Judaism. We always attended the
neighborhood orthodox synagogue on Jewish holidays.
Women were not permitted to sit and pray with the men,
so my mother and sister, Ida, sat instead in the balcony of
the synagogue. I and my brothers sat next to my father. I,
not versed in Hebrew, would read the English translation
of the Hebrew prayers printed in the book. One such
prayer stands out in my memory: "Thank you, Lord, for
having made me a man instead of a woman." At my age of
ten or so the prayer seemed to be a reasonable expression
of gratitude for being able to sit in the main section with
my father rather than sit in the gallery with my mother.

Although not devoted to Judaism, I was very devoted
to my mother and fasted with her on holiday fast days. My
brothers and I attended Hebrew school classes held in the
synagogue in the afternoon after public school classes
ended. We learned to read and write Hebrew and studied
the Torah (the Old Testament). In our home, my parents
spoke Yiddish to each other, but English was the language
of the household for their children.

Each day while my mother was preparing meals, my
father would sit at our kitchen table and read aloud from
The Forward, a popular Jewish newspaper. He also read
the Cleveland daily newspapers. We all listened to the
radio and were familiar with local and national news and
events. Father joined the Socialist Party and voted for
Norman Thomas.

Each Sunday we would listen to Father Charles E.
Coughlin, Catholic priest and pastor of the Shrine of the
Little Flower in Royal Oak, Michigan, bringing "Christ to
the Nation from Coast to Coast" on the radio. I heard with
disgust his anti-Semitic harangues and his claiming Presi-

dent Roosevelt was a Jewish communist and that Jews owned all the banks and were trying to get the country to go to war against the innocent Nazi Germany. Perhaps we listened because his misrepresentations had the positive value of making Jews seem more powerful to us than the hapless Jews being persecuted and massacred in Czarist Russia.

To supplement their meager budget, my mother worked as janitor in the building where we lived, and she also started a curtain cleaning and stretching enterprise in our home. My father worked in a clothing factory until he became ill with heart disease. Over the next twelve years my mother gave birth to four sons. I was the third, born May 11, 1922. That was the year my father had his first heart attack. He recovered and with the help of my mother was able to eke out a borderline living for his family. My siblings and I all worked at part-time jobs as soon as we were employable and able to contribute to the precarious family budget.

I found a job at age ten working Saturdays for a neighbor fruit peddler, Mr. Smolowitz. He owned an old pick-up truck which he would fill with fruits and vegetables purchased each day at a nearby farmers' market. Then he would drive in low gear up and down the neighborhood streets, calling out loudly, "Fruits and vegetables!" Housewives would emerge in answer to his call. Meanwhile he would give me boxes of fruit to carry from house to house, ringing each doorbell to sell to whomever would answer the door. On occasion he would give me strawberries to sell after placing moldy ones in the bottom of each carton and covering them with fresh alluring ones on top. My salary was one dollar plus all the leftover fruit and vegetables I could carry home. The job was not without some danger and on one occasion a spitz dog (who seemed very large at that time), leashed in front of the house that I approached, lunged at me, breaking his leash as he pounced on me and bit my leg as I scrambled to get away. The owners came out, took me to a nearby hospital emergency room where my wound was sutured. They reimbursed me for my torn trousers, but the event left me with a lifelong fear of large dogs.

Early childhood was a happy time for me as I was oblivious to my parents' struggle for survival. My brother, Bill, a year and a half younger, was my playmate and rival, endowed with superior agility and strength that overpowered me whenever we engaged in fierce but friendly wrestling. My Aunt Sarah and her husband Dave lived nearby and would visit frequently. For entertainment Uncle Dave would persuade Bill and me to wrestle, and would give five cents to the winner, who was invariably my brother who would share his winnings with me at the nearby candy store.

Our toys were meager and usually improvised, but on Christmas day, aware that Santa Claus would not be stopping at the home of his young Jewish nephews, Uncle Dave would arrive with toys and games. He was a junk peddler and owned an old horse and wagon to take him around the neighborhood seeking old throw-away metal objects, later to be sold to the city junk yard. To our delight he would occasionally let us ride bareback on his old horse in our back yard.

I was seven in 1929 when the Great Depression began and my father lost his job. One Sunday morning my mother was preparing the family breakfast. I looked at the table and saw bagels and cereal and I called out, "Ma, you forgot the cheese."

"No," she solemnly answered, "I didn't forget. Your
father is sick and not working and we just don't have
enough money for cheese."

"Oh," I said, "That means we must really be poor."

Stung by my plaintive lament, my mother silently
rushed out of the house and, to my delight, returned after
a few minutes with a package of cheddar cheese purchased at the delicatessen nearby. Too young to appreciate the extravagance of my mother's concern over my
childish complaint, I devoured the cheese, no longer
concerned about poverty. But this incident, like others to
follow, stayed with me when the time came to make
choices about the pathway my life would take.

Once when my dad was recovering from one of his
many episodes of heart failure, my mother was able to
obtain financial assistance from state welfare. A social
worker arrived soon afterwards to confirm the claim that
my father was indeed disabled and unemployable. When
she observed that he was not in bed, she questioned why
he did not return to work. My father was offended and
angrily ordered her out of our house while my mother
stood by, wringing her hands in despair over the loss of
our needed assistance.

Father, in spite of doctor's warning, opened a store-
front tailor shop in the building where we lived. His store
thrived, largely because of his skills and reputation in
repairing, altering and designing hand-made clothing. He
installed a large sign over his shop reading "Benjamin
Fierman, Tailor, CLEANING - PRESSING - ALTER-
ATION." His dream was someday to be able to change the
sign to read "Benjamin Fierman & Sons," but his dream
was never realized. I was the only one of his five sons who
had any interest in working in his tailor shop. I learned to
operate his pressing machine and received five cents for

pressing trousers and ten cents for jackets, usually done while listening to radio broadcasts of the Cleveland Indians baseball games.

My father was a gifted artisan. He made all the dress clothes for my siblings and me and was also a prominent community leader in our neighborhood, admired and respected by all who knew him. He suffered two more heart attacks over the next ten years and then was in and out of heart failure until his death at age sixty-five. Each time he would develop severe respiratory distress, my mother would hurriedly phone the local fire station staff and they would promptly arrive to administer oxygen and carry Dad by stretcher out to their van to drive him to the local hospital. After a few days on digitalis and oxygen, he would recover and return, cheerful and happy, to his home, family and tailor shop. He resisted his doctors' repeated warnings to stop smoking, but after his third heart attack and after many pleas from wife and children, he suddenly stopped. He was a great role model for me and my siblings: industrious, persevering, artistically creative in designing clothes, good-humored and fervently liberal. To this day he still appears in my dreams and thoughts, beaming, smiling and supportive. His optimistic, uncomplaining qualities have become central features of the way I try to relate to my psychotherapy patients.

Cleveland was a great city for music when I was a boy and still is. Severance Hall and the Cleveland Symphony were known world-wide. City philanthropists donated enough money to the elementary public schools to purchase instruments and develop school orchestras. I was only six and in first grade when my teacher held up in class a shiny brass mellophone (a small-sized French horn), and asked who would like to play it in the school orchestra. I raised my hand and she placed the instrument in its case and handed it to me to take to my parents to ask if they would pay for weekly lessons at fifty cents a lesson.

Carrying the heavy case I eagerly walked to my home near the school and presented my request. To my dismay my mother refused, reproaching me for not realizing that father was ill and unemployed. We were on welfare and how could I ask for such a nonessential expenditure. Chastened, I sadly went to bed after supper, hugging my instrument in bed as I went to sleep. Later I was awakened by the sounds of my mother coming into my bedroom. I pretended to be asleep and could hear her summon my father and whisper in Yiddish, "Look at that! How he loves that instrument! We must let him play it." He agreed and my lifetime music career was launched the next morning when they "surprised" me with the announcement that they would pay for my weekly lessons out of their meager budget.

I still have twinges of guilt when I recall my deception that persuaded my parents to sponsor me despite their extreme financial worries. To some extent, I rewarded their sacrifice by flourishing as a child prodigy, playing a full-sized French horn in my grade school band and orchestra, as well as in a children's chamber music quartet which performed periodically in the homes of some of the wealthy benefactors who had sponsored the schools' orchestra programs. Our performances were noted in the Cleveland Press which pictured small me with my large horn, dressed in a formal, white, flannel, double-breasted, long-trousered suit which had been made for me by my father.

I would practice my French horn daily in the back room of my Dad's tailor shop, and would end each hour by playing the song of the Volga Boatmen for him to join in and sing the Russian lyrics in his baritone voice. Then he would reward me with a nickel which I usually spent for an ice cream cone. I also competed in city-wide school music competitions and frequently won first prize in the horn contests.

In grade school my interests evolved from music to math, literature and science. I began to read books with a passion, each day bringing home one or two from the school library. Stories of Robin Hood, King Arthur, Ivanhoe, Captain Horatio Hornblower, Moby Dick, Sherlock Holmes, etc., filled all my free time. No television then to compete with my reading.

Our home was a bustling crowded haven for my parents and their five sons and one daughter, each pursuing their own interests and dreams, but all committed to the family's welfare. My sister, Ida, thirteen years older than I, was a beautiful, spirited girl who at age nineteen entered and won a Clara Bow look-alike competition. Clara Bow was a "flapper," the "It Girl," a popular sexy movie actress in the 20s. Ida went on to win a second contest, the Miss Forward Beauty Contest sponsored by the Jewish newspaper, *The Forward*. After graduating from high school she obtained a job as an operator for the city telephone company and kept that job until retirement in her sixties. She and her husband, Frank Reminick, a life-time postal clerk, lived in an apartment on the shore of Lake Erie and occasionally took me into their apartment during summer vacations to relieve my mother's crowded household. Her husband had a noteworthy life history in that at age nine he and his mother and young sister were scheduled to sail steerage from Liverpool, England to Ellis Island, New York on the Titanic, but were prevented from boarding because his mother was found to have an eye infection. The Titanic sailed without them and sank with much loss of life. Days later, after his mother's infection healed, they sailed steerage successfully to America on another ship. Ida and Frank had three children who eventually gave them ten grandchildren who in turn gave them eighteen great-grandchildren. She lived bravely until she died at age ninety-three.

My brother, Isadore (Izzy), ten years older than I, was a serious, hard working door-to-door salesman after his graduation from high school. He married Elaine, a beautiful department store saleslady. We grieved with them when their firstborn baby girl died of sudden infant death syndrome (SIDS). Later they had two healthy children. Isadore died suddenly at age fifty-nine of a heart attack.

My brother, Joseph (Joey), was a cheerful, friendly young man who drove a car to pick up and deliver clothing to my father's customers. At technical school he became interested in printing and after graduation bought a used manual printing press which he installed in the back room of my father's tailor shop. He taught me to hand-feed his printing press while he solicited printing orders from local merchants and stores. Within a few months he had enough paying clients to afford more printing equipment and open a printing shop in downtown Cleveland. He married and over the years had five children. Unfortunately, his wife, Sylvia, died of fatal complications in the attempted delivery of her sixth child. Joe was devastated and moved with his children into my parents' home. My mother, having raised her own six children took over the mothering of her five motherless grandchildren, ages five to twelve. I and my siblings had to double up in beds at night and my parents had a small room built in our basement for me to have a place to study and do my school homework.

My brother, Frank, three years older, was displaced as baby of the family when I was born, only to be displaced a year and a half later by the birth of my younger brother, William (Bill). Frank was ill as a child with a spinal deformity that required him to be in a body cast and to be in and out of hospitals during our early years of life. My childhood, spent living in a crowded home, sharing family joys but feeling helpless and anguished when stress and illness affected my parents and siblings, all left me with a sense of being an unnecessary burden to my harassed parents. I believe that pervasive feeling of guilt in my childhood became a prime motive for me to seek a life and career of relieving the suffering of others as a physician, a psychiatrist and a psychotherapist.

My parents were role models for me and I loved them both very much. Their dedication and commitment to their children's welfare; their industriousness; their recognition that education was the way their children could escape from the poverty and constrictions of their own lives; their bravery in facing and overcoming the hardships involved in emigrating to a new and challenging country and culture; their love of music; their unconditional love and support for their children—all of which set a pattern of being for me that continued throughout my life.

2

TEENAGER

2

TEENAGER

During the fourteenth century, rabbis formalized the tradition that at age thirteen a Jewish boy becomes old enough to participate as an adult in all ceremonies, rituals, and practices of Judaism. They did so by introducing the ceremony of *Bar Mitzvah* ("man of duty") in which a Jewish lad on or about his thirteenth birthday attends his synagogue to read to the assembled congregation that day's section from the Torah (The Old Testament), and then pledges his commitment to Judaism. So it was for me on the sunny morning of my thirteenth birthday to be accompanied by my proud and beaming parents and siblings to our small neighborhood synagogue where, draped in a fringed prayer shawl *(tallis)* and wearing a silk skullcap *(yarmulka)*, I was called to the altar by the rabbi. There I read aloud in Hebrew to the assemblage the required segment in the Torah. Then in English I pledged that as a full-fledged "adult" member ("Today, I am a man,") of the 4000-year-old, world-wide Jewish community, I would assume all the religious and ethical obligations of Jewish life. After the ceremony a celebration was held in my home, where I received gifts from friends and relatives, including several proverbial fountain pens. I acknowledged the gifts by announcing to the dismay of my family, "Today, I am a fountain pen!"

While I enjoyed my *Bar Mitzvah* and the feeling that I now "belonged," the truth was that without denying my Jewish birth, identity and heritage, I had become more and more alienated from orthodox Jewish beliefs and teaching. I began reading about Christianity, Buddhism and the Muslim religion and was impressed with the similarities of these religions with the ethical beliefs of Judaism. But none of the alleged revelations and events described in the texts were convincing to me. I found it hard to believe that any mature, intelligent and educated person would hold such superstitious beliefs.

However, I could appreciate that religious beliefs had relieved fears and anxieties that have tormented people through the ages in regard to the mysteries of creation, the universe, birth, life and death. But I felt I could live with these mysteries unsolved without relying on fictitious answers that border on the absurd. Atheism became my "religion" and I agreed with the whimsical quip, "Faith is when you believe in something that no one in their right mind would ever believe in." Out of respect for my parents I withheld my atheism from them and participated fully in their observances of Jewish holidays and practices. From time to time I would discuss my disbelief with siblings and friends and found that while most of them shared my concerns, they preferred to position themselves as agnostics rather than as atheists. I would then tease them by declaring, "An agnostic is really a cowardly atheist!"

My teenage life was rife with concerns about family, music, school, friendships, Judaism, anti-Semitism, sports, girls and sex. My dad was an inspiring role model for me—hard working, conscientious, good-natured, cheerful and non-complaining despite chronic coronary artery disease, diabetes and Buerger's disease (chronic painful inflammation of the arteries in the legs). His poor health was always a cloud over my childhood and teenage years. My mother was robust, devout, healthy and industrious, raising her six children with a firm hand and anxiously tending to my dad's needs whenever his health worsened. Despite borderline poverty, they stressed maximum education for all their children; but only my brother, Frank, and I achieved graduate degrees; my brother in group social work and I in medicine and psychiatry. I admired and loved my parents and have tried to make their admirable qualities the mainstays of my own personhood in dealing with people and with life.

Throughout my early childhood I felt isolated in my relationships with my parents and five siblings. The household was crowded and there was always someone seriously ill. I felt "out of the loop" and detached from the stresses and struggles of my parents and older siblings. I even felt my parents had erred in giving birth to me and my younger brother, Bill, in view of the hardships in their lives. However, any feelings of being neglected by my parents were overcome once they acknowledged and took pride in my achievements in school and music, and my Dad was pleased when I asked him to teach me how to press clothes on his pressing machine so that I could help him in his small tailor shop. By the time I was thirteen, my sister, Ida, and my older brothers, Isadore and Joseph, were all married and living separately. Frank, only three years older, and Bill, one year younger, both became close friends of mine throughout their lives.

Despite my avid interest in reading, I was no book-worm nerd and was very active socially with several friends throughout my adolescence. Six of us formed a boys' club at the local Jewish community center and we competed with other clubs in athletics, basketball and baseball. We called ourselves the "Cain-Lo" Club, mean-ing in Hebrew, the "Yes-No" club, the "Yes" was for house parties and dancing with teenage girls' clubs, and the "No" referred to alcohol, drugs and juvenile crime. Soli-tary dating was unusual for boys and girls in the 30s, and was regarded as "going steady" and having a serious exclusive relationship. But house parties served as oppor-tunities for introducing club members to teenage hetero-sexual behavior. Frenetic dancing, spin-the-bottle, and surreptitious kissing and groping frequently occurred when chaperones were lax or absent. Adolescent hor-mones were not to be denied and neither was sex-related rivalry.

On one occasion the Cain-Lo Club was invited to a Catholic girl's house party. On arriving near the girl's home, we were accosted by a group of belligerent teenage boys loudly calling us "Kikes" and warning us that we were encroaching on their turf and on their girlfriends. The warnings escalated to cursing, shoving, punching and kicking when, luckily, the girls came out of the house and exhorted their male "friends" to disperse. They withdrew shouting, "We'll get you Kikes when you come out!"

The violence outside in no way discouraged the lively party inside. Later that evening the attractive hostess danced with me and then led me to an empty room for some aggressive kissing and necking. But as we embraced, I could see out the window that a lynch mob of youths, including her boyfriend, was waiting for us in the street. I felt I was receiving the kiss of death made famous by the Mafia, plus mouth-to-mouth resuscitation in advance. I pulled away, gulped and croaked, "Susan, do you think you could call your father or brother to drive us guys home in his van?" Susan laughed, but agreed.

In school the world of science began to open for me. Finding through science how things worked captured my imagination. I excelled in math, chemistry and physics, but I was also devoted to the school orchestra and marching band. In high school I was principal horn player for its symphony orchestra. Beethoven, Mozart, Brahms, Tchaikovsky and Wagner became my new heroes. I won first place in Cleveland's high school French horn solo competitions. The John Adams orchestra won the Ohio state high school orchestra competition and we were invited to the national competition held in Riverside, California. The Cleveland Press sponsored a city-wide drive to raise funds to pay for the trip for the fifty students in the orchestra, but the parents of each student were required to pay fifty dollars as well. My parents could not afford that, so the orchestra's conductor reluctantly had to ask the school to pay for me. He did so because he could not find another student who could play well enough to replace me.

Throughout my high school years my conductor had displayed a mean-spirited attitude towards me which, rightly or wrongly, I ascribed to anti-Semitism. On one occasion, when I was late for the marching band's morning drill, I was extremely embarrassed to be greeted by him with a loud scornful sneer, "So you're late again! Was it because you were too busy chewing on your pork rinds for breakfast?" I was too fearful and intimidated to respond angrily to him, and my love of playing music in his orchestra kept me from quitting. Besides, I had no idea what "pork rinds" were, other than that I was sure no Jewish boy would ever want to eat them.

We placed third in the national competition in California, and on our train trip home we stopped to tour the spectacular Grand Canyon. "Golly, what a gully!" I quipped to my orchestra friends' amusement and to our conductor's annoyance. On returning home I was shocked to find he had given me a failing grade of F in music. "That's for being late so many times for our rehearsals," he scornfully explained. I pleaded with him in vain to change the grade because failing would prevent me from being elected to the school Honor Society.

Fortunately, my older brother, Frank, a graduate of the school, informed me of a rule that prevented any teacher from failing a student without having given prior notice to the parents that their child was failing. My brother and I went to the school principal with this knowledge and my grade was raised to a D. Not quite an acquittal, but enough for me to gain access to the Honor Society.

At my graduation, the orchestra played the overture to the Prince Igor opera by Aleksandr Borodin, a piece that included a difficult French horn solo. My proud parents were in the audience and I was inspired to play better than ever before. As we broke up to join our parents, the conductor singled me out and snarled, "If you had played that way in California, we would have won first place!"

But what to do after graduation? Western Reserve University in Cleveland offered a few scholarships for high school seniors to be awarded on the basis of a written competitive examination. I won one of the scholarships and planned to begin college that fall with a major in chemistry. I chose chemistry as my major because I believed that a bachelor's degree in chemistry was a definitive degree that would enable me to become employed as a chemist.

I had also considered making music my career. All through my school years I had played school French horns but did not own one and lacked funds to buy one. The United States Marine Band did not answer my letter offering to enlist. However, the Ohio State National Guard did have a band stationed in Cleveland, and I enlisted in order to play their French horn. We rehearsed weekends in the city armory, wore army uniforms, played at state formal gatherings and marched at parades. The band conductor was a colonel in the National Guard who welcomed me as the only French horn player in his band. His civilian job was as a driver of a large gasoline tanker truck, and he knew I was hoping to begin college in the fall.

The year was 1940. German armies were overwhelming Europe. FDR was running for re-election for an unprecedented third term as president. America was preparing for the possibility of becoming embroiled in the war in Europe, which, in fact, happened the following year after Japan bombed Pearl Harbor on December 7, 1941. The Draft law had been passed and I had graduated from John Adams High School in Cleveland, Ohio in 1940. "Where do I go from here?" I wondered; father ill, family struggling to make ends meet; no money, no connections. Yet, despite all odds, I set my sights on college and chemistry as a career.

To earn money to contribute to my family's meager income, I answered an ad from a hardware store seeking a clerk. The owner informed me that the job included driving his Model T Ford for home deliveries and installing home appliances. "Can you drive?" he asked. "Yes," I lied, feeling sure I would be able teach myself to drive since I had been a frequent passenger in cars driven by my older siblings and relatives, and I had observed many times how they handled the manual shifts in their cars.

After a few days at work, I was given the keys to the car and told to make my first delivery. I knew there was a cemetery nearby and managed to drive there with the car in first gear. To my dismay the entry to the cemetery was at the top of a hill and the car began rolling downhill rapidly. I tried stomping on the clutch hoping it was the brake, which it wasn't. In a panic I jumped out of the car and watched as it careened downhill until it drove into a large bush and stopped. I walked down to the car thankful that no collision with tombstones had occurred and then I practiced driving until I had mastered all the shifts and foot pedals. I drove all that summer without a license.

One day as I was walking along the uphill street next to the store where I worked, I heard a loud grinding noise behind me. I turned and was amazed to see a large tanker truck backing up slowly and noisily up the narrow street with the driver's arm waving up and down out of his window. When the truck came closer I could see that the driver was my National Guard band conductor trying to get my attention. I ran up to the window and he called out, "Lou, if you still want to go to college this fall you better resign from the Guard right now. I've just learned that there's a plan to activate the National Guard into the U.S. Army!" I thanked him profusely for his concern about me and that week I quit the National Guard and its band and resigned myself to a life without a French horn. I learned later that the Ohio National Guard did see combat against the Nazis in Europe.

In September, I told my boss I was quitting to begin undergraduate studies at Cleveland College of Western Reserve University. To my surprise, he became upset and pleaded that I continue working for him with the promise that in time he would make me a partner in his business. I gratefully declined.

My older brother, Frank, working his way through graduate school in group social work, had a midnight job as nurse's aide in the university hospital. He was able to arrange for me to work there also as a nurse's aide on his same midnight shift. This was my first experience and exposure to the intense drama of hospital life. I was very impressed with the dedication of the hospital staff responsible for the care of patients suffering from pain, life-threatening injuries and illnesses; interns, nurses and attending physicians all making weighty decisions affecting life and death outcomes. I had never before considered that I might have the competence and resources to seek a medical career, but now I felt attracted to the idea.

A memorable experience reinforced my growing interest in a medical career. I can recall vividly the ward nurse calling out, "Fierman! Get to Room 113 and stay with that patient until he's dead!" Stunned by the order, I obeyed without question. The patient was a sixty-year-old tramp who had lived alone in a shack on the city's lake front. It was alleged that he was an alcoholic who had set fire to his bed while drinking and smoking that night. He suffered third degree burns over most of his body and was not expected to live through the night. He was in coma, swathed in bandages, breathing slowly and noisily. I had never seen a dying person before other than in the movies. I was sent to be with him because it was hospital practice not to let patients die alone. The rationale of this policy was never explained to me. After an hour or so his breathing became softer and slower and gradually stopped completely. His final gurgling breath seemed to last a long time. I became increasingly anxious at his bedside, staring at what I believed to be the final exodus of a human spirit. When he stopped breathing, I could feel his unseen presence in the room as a spirit outside of his body standing close to me. I panicked and rushed out of the room calling to the nurse, "He's dead!" As the nurse approached, I cautiously re-entered the room and no longer felt the presence of his spirit. The nurse and I wrapped the body, placed "it" on a stretcher, and I pushed it to the hospital morgue. I was shaken, perplexed and unsettled. Had I really experienced a real spirit—the departing soul of a dying human being?

Later I confided my moving experience to my brother, Frank, and told him of my admiration for the hospital staff and asked his advice about seeking a medical career. He was very enthusiastic and supportive and urged me to switch my major from chemistry to pre-med and promised to help find the money for tuition if and when I was accepted into a medical school.

The highlights of my college years consisted of my straight-A, pre-med class work, my nighttime job as nurse's aide, and my courtship of my classmate, Ella Yensen. Ella was an eighteen-year-old psychology major of remarkable beauty and intellect who had won the same competitive scholarship as I had. Her picture appeared on the front page of *The Cleveland Press* when it announced the winners of the contest. I was visiting with my best friend, Phillip Perloff, when the newspaper arrived, and, pointing to her picture, I declared excitedly, "There's the girl I'm going to marry!"

At college I contacted her and she agreed to date, but, as we became close friends, she warned that she intended to devote her life to academic pursuits and would never marry. My orthodox Jewish mother became increasingly worried about my close friendship with Ella, who came from a Christian Science background. Mother was extremely fearful that I would marry outside the Jewish faith, but she was relieved when I promised her that this would not happen. She even became friendly with Ella, who frequently visited our home for us to study together for our classes.

By my twentieth birthday, my life had settled down to a routine of working at the university hospital from midnight to 8:00 AM; college classes from 8:00 AM to 4:00 PM; and home from 4:00 PM to midnight. My resolve to pursue a career in medicine was encouraged by my doing well in college chemistry, biology and physiology. But I had a competing resolve to pursue my courtship of Ella. I felt I had found my soulmate and we became inseparable, despite differences in goals and religious affiliation. My Jewish atheism did not fit well with her Christian Science beliefs and we argued over a wide spectrum of issues. But she had access to her sister's car for our dates to movies, theaters, concerts and sports events. We shared expenses and I was resigned to her declaration that a future marriage was not an option for us.

During World War II I was on Enlisted Reserve status with the Draft Board as long as I was in college, but as we became seniors we had to face separation. She planned to apply to some out-of-state graduate schools, while I decided to apply to the Western Reserve University School of Medicine in Cleveland, Ohio.

3

THANK YOU, DOCTOR ARROWSMITH

3

THANK YOU, DOCTOR ARROWSMITH

As a teenager I had read *Arrowsmith*, a novel by Sinclair Lewis about a heroic young doctor who pursues his life's goal of science, research and medicine despite many daunting obstacles. I admired his perseverance and was determined to follow his inspiring example; but how? How to get into medical school and how to find the money for tuition? No government loans were available in those days; medicine was a rich boy's career. But first I had to be accepted by a medical school. In my junior year in college, I applied for admission to Western Reserve University School of Medicine in Cleveland, Ohio

I was interviewed by Dean Sollman, a famed professor of pharmacology. He explained unabashedly that although my grades were top-notch, and I was clearly well qualified, I would not be accepted because the school had already accepted its "quota" of Jewish students, namely, four out of the hundred students admitted each year, matching the four percent Jews in the population of Cleveland!

In the 1940s, the quota system for admission of Jewish students to graduate schools was commonplace, widespread and passively accepted, and it would be many years before that policy would finally be banned. I sat there listening quietly to the Dean's explanation, which now, on reflection, rouses anger and the thought, "What a pompous, condescending, anti-Semitic bigot!" However, at that time I just accepted his explanation without protest. Nor did I ask him to explain why his percentage system did not apply as well to Blacks or women, since none of them were accepted at all.

My applications to Ohio State University and the University of Cincinnati were rejected without interviews, and I assumed their "quotas" were also filled. Since I could not finance an out-of-state medical school, I became resigned to being called on graduation into active service in the U.S. Army. To my great surprise and intense delight, a notice arrived from Western Reserve University one month before the beginning of the next term announcing that I had been accepted after all. Thank you, Doctor Arrowsmith! Apparently, one of the four Jewish students previously accepted decided to go elsewhere and I had been next on the quota list. How amazing! However, I had to face the next challenge that required I pay the full first year's tuition ($500) in advance. Doctor Arrowsmith! Where was I to find the money for the tuition?

My brother, Frank, who had persuaded me to change my major in college from chemistry to pre-med, promised that following his graduation from the School of Social Work he would help me obtain the tuition for medical school if I were accepted. To my dismay, as soon as he graduated he married and left Cleveland to take a social work position in Indianapolis, Indiana.

"Frank! How can you do this to me!" I thought, but before his leaving he provided me with a list of ten alleged Jewish philanthropists in Cleveland, assuring me that at least one of them would help me with the money I needed for tuition. Hat in hand, I saw them all but was turned down one by one, usually because of their own alleged financial problems.

One woman on the list, a wealthy elderly widow, offered to subsidize me if I would agree to train for a career as a rabbi! "Too many doctors," she proclaimed, "Not enough rabbis!" "Thanks," I stammered, "but I could not do that." Had my muse, Doctor Arrowsmith, abandoned me? The tenth and final philanthropist on my list referred me to Doctor Harold Goldblatt, a famed professor of pathology at Western Reserve, known for his discovery of a major cause of hypertension. Doctor Goldblatt praised my college record and two weeks later summoned me to his office to hand me a check from an anonymous donor for my first year's tuition! My faith in my muse was restored! Thank you, Doctor Arrowsmith! On my graduation from medical school, Dr. Goldblatt informed me that my generous benefactor was a Mr. Silver, an industrialist in Cleveland whose only condition for the grant was that I pledge to help other medical students in financial need in the future, which I have since been privileged to do.

My joy over receiving a grant for my first year's tuition was tempered by my need for additional funds to cover my personal living expenses. I noticed a newspaper ad from a local funeral director seeking someone to work evenings and nights at his funeral home which was conveniently located near the medical school. I applied and was hired. The home was a grand, spacious two-storied house on

Cleveland's Euclid Avenue and had previously housed the family of the owner of the White Sewing Machine Company. The funeral director now lived with his family on the second floor and maintained his funeral business on the main floor. The spacious first floor was ringed by caskets on display plus offices and rooms for funeral and memorial services. In the basement were rooms for embalming bodies and also a crematorium.

My duties were to work each day from 5:00 PM to 7:00 AM the following morning, six days a week. The Director would decide each week what day I would have off from work. I was to live and work in an office on the first floor which contained a desk and chairs, small refrigerator, cot for sleeping, private bathroom and a telephone with a very loud amplified ring. My job was to answer the phone at all hours of the night and take messages which were usually about deaths. If funeral arrangements were requested, I would then call the driver of the funeral home's hearse to bring the body, and finally I would summon the embalmer.

I did not inform anyone at medical school since I knew the officials frowned on students taking outside jobs, but the salary was necessary for me and I later found that my hours at work were frequently undisturbed by any calls, permitting me to pursue fully my medical studies. The only proviso was that I was never to leave the house, permitting the Director and his family to be free and undisturbed by calls six evenings a week.

The embalmer, Mr. Donahue, was friendly and invited me to watch his work. He was very efficient and creative in preparing the bodies for display to their families and mourners. He was artistic in applying cosmetics and confided to me that his wife even had him put her make-up on her when they socialized. On the bodies he used staplers and padding to secure neatly the facial structures including the eyes and jaw, but his embalming technique was gruesome. Like Captain Ahab harpooning Moby Dick, Mr. Donahue, using a hollow harpoon-like spear connected to a huge vat filled with formaldehyde, would pierce the abdomen of the body and infuse the internal cavities of the chest and abdomen with formaldehyde. He then would connect the vat to major arteries and veins and flush out all the blood with more formaldehyde. Observing him at work was morbidly fascinating, but the knowledge proved useful later when, as an intern, I was required to obtain permission from surviving relatives to have an autopsy performed on their deceased family member. Their resistance frequently was promoted by their undertaker telling them that their loved one's body would be mutilated by the autopsy. When I explained that the hospital pathologist's autopsy would be a respectful surgical procedure, compared to their own undertaker emulating Captain Ahab, the relatives would usually give their consent.

The funeral home also had facilities for cremation of the body of the deceased as an option for the relatives. I would assist Mr. Donahue in placing the body onto a slab that would then slide into the crematorium. After he ignited the burning flames, I was able to watch through an opening in the door and could see that the body inside would respond to the intense heat by partially sitting up as it was being devoured by the fierce flames. In later years learning of the horrors of the Holocaust, I could visualize the dreadful cremation of the bodies of millions of Jews murdered by the Nazis.

Despite the restrictions that my daily evening job placed on my limited time for recreation and socialization, my friendship with Ella continued unabated. Ella agreed to visit me frequently at the funeral home and would bring sandwiches, snacks and soda. My small radio provided music for us to dance by in the large first-floor room surrounded by an array of coffins on display.

On the first day of medical school in September of 1944 there was a social get-acquainted gathering for all freshman students. I looked about with trepidation at the well-dressed, lively group of classmates, all white males in their early twenties, appearing confident, clearly affluent, bright and eager. I felt burdened by my Jewish minority status and having poor immigrant parents who were unable to raise the money needed for my first year's tuition. Soon I was drawn into the interactions of the group where the most frequent topic of discussion was concern with the occupations of our fathers. Bankers, lawyers, doctors and business tycoons were frequently cited professions of the fathers of many of my fellow classmates. Finally, the dreaded question was put to me. "And what does your dad do, Lou?"

I hesitated to answer because I felt ashamed to admit to my upper-class colleagues that my father was a simple tailor whose small shop barely eked out enough income to support his wife and six children. Suddenly I thought of the large sign my father had placed over the door to his tailor shop, boldly declaring his services; namely, "CLEANING, PRESSING and ALTERATION."

"Oh," I finally answered my interrogator, "he's a CPA."

"An accountant! Great!" my new-found friend exclaimed. And so it was for the duration of my medical school experience. With each new inquiry about my father I would elaborate on his fictitious career as a certified public accountant. But the emotional price paid for this deception has been heavy and my private shame over denying my father's profession has lasted to this day. I deeply regret that I lacked the courage to present my father honestly to my classmates that day in 1944.

Later that year I quit my funeral home job when to my great joy and relief, all my financial and tuition problems were solved by the U.S. Army taking over medical schools throughout the country in order to speed up its training of doctors for the Medical Corps during World War II. The program was called the Army Specialist Training Program (ASTP) and all medical students were enlisted in the Army as salaried active-duty privates. We wore army uniforms, marched to and from classes, drilled on school campus and, since all vacations were canceled, completed the four-year curriculum in three years.

On one memorable occasion I was painfully reminded of the social and political differences that separated the ninety-six wealthy, upper-class, Christian, probably Republican students from the four middle-class, Jewish, probably Democratic students. On April 12, 1945, as we were all seated in our amphitheater classroom, taking notes as our professor of forensic medicine was lecturing, a female secretary entered and handed a written note to the professor and then turned and left. He stared at the note for a long minute, looked up and announced, "I have just been informed that President Roosevelt has just had a stroke and has died! Class is dismissed for the rest of the day." He turned and quickly left the room as pandemonium broke out. All but four students leaped from their seats, joyously threw their army caps into the air, danced around the amphitheater steps and on the floor, shouting, "Hooray! Hooray! The Great White Father is dead!" In contrast, the four Jewish students remained seated, transfixed, speechless and teary-eyed. Roosevelt had been my president ever since I was ten and was regarded by me and my family as our country's great war-time leader. I regarded my dancing soldier-classmates celebrating the death of their commander-in-chief as disgusting ingrates and traitorous low-lifes.

Despite contempt for my right-wing classmates, medical school was a delight, a dream come true. Each subject and each medical specialty, including psychiatry, was entrancing to me. I recall vividly my first day in anatomy dissection class. All the students were divided into teams of four and each team was assigned to a cadaver on a stretcher covered with a sheet, ready for dissection. The professor teaching the class began the session by solemnly warning, "Remember, just as you are respectful to patients when they are alive, you must be respectful to their bodies when they are dead. You all have your Gray's Anatomy textbook and your instructions for dissection, so please begin." As the teams removed the sheets covering the bodies, I could hear noises in the room sounding "thump-thump-thump...." I looked about and was amazed to see that three of the students in the room had fainted and fallen flat on their backs on the floor. They were quickly revived and were embarrassed as they explained that they had never been so close to a dead body before. Of course, this was not true for me. Apparently, none of my classmates had spent evenings dancing in funeral homes or watching embalmers at work.

The bodies, mainly those of unclaimed dead paupers, were sent to the medical school by police and hospitals. Social Security or welfare programs paying for funerals were not available in the 1940s, so these bodies were used for training and research, and their remains after dissection were buried in a pauper's grave. On a few occasions, additional bodies were donated to the medical school by concerned individuals who left instructions in their wills.

In my course on operative surgery, the same teams of students from the anatomy class were each assigned a dog to be used by the team to perform a series of weekly surgical operations. None of the scheduled operations were life-threatening, and the challenge for each team was to keep its dog alive throughout the course. The professor instructing the course was an elderly retired surgeon who was afflicted with Parkinson's Disease. He was also assigned a dog to demonstrate the various operations the teams were to perform on their dogs. Although he had significant rest tremors (shaking), he did not have any so-called intention tremors, and was able to make firm, steady incisions with his scalpel. On the first day of class while he was demonstrating how to make a lengthy simple incision on the abdomen of his anesthetized dog, once again the sounds of students fainting and falling on the floor were heard as soon as they observed red blood welling up in the wound inflicted on the dog. Once revived, the demonstration continued. That memory is still with me whenever I hear the time-worn joking definition of a psychiatrist as being "a Jewish doctor who cannot stand the sight of blood!"

Each week my team performed the required operation on our dog, a mixed hound we named Pluto. Each student rotated through the positions of anesthetist, principal surgeon, assistant surgeon and surgical nurse. My turn as principal surgeon was to remove one of Pluto's kidneys, which I was proud to do successfully. Pluto survived all the operations and was returned to the medical school in good health, hopefully to have a well deserved retirement.

The three years of medical school passed quickly. Each subject and each specialty was intensely interesting except for public health and psychiatry. The public health course focused on water, food control and epidemiology while psychiatry was taught by a neurologist as a subspecialty of internal medicine. I barely scanned those textbooks and studied only long enough to pass the final examinations. Little did I dream that in the future I would be arbitrarily appointed by the Army Medical Corps to be a Military Government Public Health Officer. Nor did I anticipate that psychiatry would ever become my final career choice.

All my interactions with students, faculty, hospital personnel and patients were lively and congenial with one notable exception. My only traumatic negative experience occurred one day in my pathology class. The hospital's pathology amphitheater was used not only for lectures but also for the administration of written exams. We sat in alternate seats at the direction of the pathology professor, a scowling, domineering, critical teacher, known both for his research and his ill temper. The test papers were passed out and we all began to write out the answers to the difficult questions.

"You there!" a harsh shout broke the silence of the room. I looked up and to my dismay saw the professor pointing at me. "Come down here and sit in the front row!" "Why?" I timidly asked. "You know why!" he snarled. All my classmates were staring at me and I realized I was being falsely accused of cheating by looking at the test papers of classmates seated below me! My anger flared up and I declared defiantly, "There's no reason for me to do that!"

"Come down immediately or else turn in your paper!" he demanded. I blushed, furious at the implication that I was cheating and was determined to not move. My friend seated near me called out, "Do it! Go down, Lou. He means it!" I sat rigid and silent. I knew my grade would suffer severely if I did not submit, but I was determined not to give in. "You have thirty seconds to come down!" my nemesis grated. After several seconds silently passed, I stood up and with shame and fury I slowly walked down to the first row and sat down to finish the examination. When done I walked over to the professor and handed him my paper and started to protest my innocence. He turned his back on me and spurned my attempt to deny any cheating. He was not the professor in any of my other classes and I never had words with him again, but the bitter memory of my surrendering to an undeserved humiliation has haunted me ever since.

Upon graduation in 1946 the members of my class were all commissioned as Lieutenants in the U.S. Army Medical Corps, and given a one-year leave from active duty to have an internship. Due to my indecisiveness about specializing I chose to have a rotating internship at Cleveland City Hospital, including psychiatry. As an intern on psychiatry my duties were to examine and medicate patients admitted to the psychiatry wards. I was intrigued by the delusional paranoid schizophrenics and the bizarre catatonic patients. Psychotherapy was done by senior residents who also administered electroconvulsive shock therapy and insulin coma therapy.

On one occasion I was told to suture the wound of a young catatonic woman who had slashed her wrist with a piece of glass before assuming a stiff, frozen-like, mute, staring, unresponsive posture. When she didn't acknowledge or respond to my presence, I now confess with shame that I sadistically decided to test her catatonia by not using any local anesthetic unless and until she either responded to me or to the pain of being sutured. My cruel experiment failed when she remained stiff, silent and immobile despite my needle penetrating her skin for the many sutures needed to close her wound. It was only years later that I learned that people in altered states of consciousness can also block the sensation of pain.

The surgical specialties were very appealing to me. The drama of operative interventions into the structure and functions of the body was very exciting. Most of my time on surgery was spent holding retractors during operations performed by senior residents and attending surgeons and watching their scrupulous care and caution as they made their exquisite incisions with their scalpels. But there was tragedy as well as triumph for the residents to observe and experience. On one occasion an eight-year-old child undergoing a routine tonsillectomy had a sudden unexpected cardiac arrest and died despite all frantic efforts of the surgical team to resuscitate him. I accompanied the surgeon as he brought the dreadful news to the parents who were devastated with grief.

Another memorable experience for me was the application of postoperative care to a thirty-year-old man who had been brought to the emergency room of the hospital by police. We were told the patient had a history of previous psychotic episodes, and had on this occasion gone to his church with an ax and while kneeling on the door steps, positioned his penis on a step and chopped it off with his ax. A priest rushed out, retrieved the penis and both patient and penis were rushed to the hospital for surgery. The urological surgeon meticulously and painstakingly restored the penis and for a week afterwards my daily task was to clean the wound and change the dressing. I sadly watched as the penis gradually lost its structural and vascular continuity with the patient's body, became increasingly dark and shriveled, finally dropping off, leaving a small but intact and functional remnant of his penis.

I was moved by the entire sequence of events and engaged the patient frequently about his behavior and his history. The patient, who was extremely lucid, rational and communicative, explained that he blamed his penis for being responsible for his sinful, sexual thoughts and urges. As a devout Catholic he struggled with his guilt-ridden desire to masturbate, finally deciding to emasculate himself. The attending psychiatrist explained to me that it was not uncommon for schizophrenic patients to become temporarily lucid and free of psychotic speech and behavior immediately after committing an act of violence, either towards themselves or others.

My worst surgical experience was my participation in a failed attempt by a gynecologist to save a young pregnant woman's life by performing a so-called late-term abortion which involves terminating the life of the baby in order to extract it immediately from the uterus. The woman was in her first pregnancy, but in labor she had developed sudden life-threatening eclampsia and coma. Emergency measures including the drastic abortion had to be performed, but all efforts failed and she died. Again, I had to convey the tragic news to the husband and comfort him in the waiting room.

While on the surgical service I considered becoming a surgeon, but when assigned to perform minor surgery on superficial wounds in the Emergency Room, I proved to be extremely anxious and cautious. I can still hear my supervising resident surgeon shouting, "Fierman! Are you still working on that wound? You should have been done a long time ago!" The patient, needless to say, looked quite uneasy at having me sew up his wounds. I decided surgery was not meant to be the specialty of choice for me and I chose internal medicine instead.

4

TAI-I SAN OISHA-SAN FIERMAN-SAN
(Captain Doctor Fierman)

4

TAI-I SAN OISHA-SAN FIERMAN-SAN
(Captain Doctor Fierman)

In 1945, WWII ended with the unconditional surrender of Japan, but for all the Army Specialist Training Program (ASTP) doctors, two more years of active military service would still be required following graduation from medical school and completion of internship. Thus, in 1947, at age 25, after completing a rotating internship in Cleveland, Ohio, I was ordered to report to Fort Sam Houston in San Antonio, Texas for one month of basic training as a Lieutenant in the U.S. Army Medical Corps. While I regretted leaving family, friends and Ella, my "steady" girlfriend in Cleveland, I felt gratitude to my country for freely providing the bulk of my medical school training and I was proud to be part of the U.S. military that had so brilliantly defeated the evil axis of Hitler's Germany, Mussolini's Italy and Hirohito's Japan. Two years of obligatory military service seemed to be a small price for me to pay in return.

In sunny Texas I joined hundreds of young uniformed army physicians, all of whom had just completed their internship. We were housed in large air-conditioned barracks and scheduled for daily lectures on disease control and food and water inspection, plus daily drills and vigorous physical fitness exercise. There was little time for socializing or recreation, but movies were provided and we did have time to visit the Alamo and nearby Laredo, Mexico.

As the weeks passed, we were all asked to rank in order which military theater of action we preferred for assignment. The choices were: Stateside, Europe, Central America, Alaska, Hawaii, the Philippines or the Orient. My first choice was Stateside, my last was the Orient, but consistent with the inscrutable nature of the military mind, I received orders to report in one week to San Francisco, California for shipment by boat to an assignment in Japan. However, we were also informed that wives would be permitted to join their husbands in their assigned military location. Unfortunately for me, this offer was not extended to girl friends or fiancees, but the Army also announced that if any of the single doctors present wished to marry before leaving Fort Sam Houston, they would be provided with a military wedding in the Fort's chapel, including a military chaplain and an honor guard of soldiers with raised sabers plus a wedding night in the posh officers' bridal suite.

Faced with a two-year separation from the woman I loved, I decided to phone Ella and propose a military marriage at the Fort, even though it meant breaking the promise I had made seven years before to my mother that I would never marry outside the Jewish faith. Ella refused my proposal. I left the Fort and flew back to Cleveland and was able to persuade her to marry so as to be eligible to join me in Japan.

My mother became extremely distraught and agitated on learning about our plans. She pleaded with me to change my mind and tearfully threatened to disown me if I refused, consistent with her orthodox Judaic beliefs. I was saddened but not surprised when my father joined my mother in censuring me, but I was not to be deterred by what I regarded as archaic religious nonsense.

With only a few days left to report to Army headquarters in San Francisco, Ella and I agreed to marry in a small Protestant church in her neighborhood in Lyndhurst, Ohio. When we entered the church to make arrangements with the local pastor, I was confronted by a wall-to-wall, ceiling-to-floor, gold-colored crucifix painted at the end of the church. As we walked down the central aisle, the crucifix seemed to pulsate and I became dizzy, felt weakness in my legs, cardiac palpitations, shortness of breath, sweating and a sense of impending doom! "Ella!" I gasped, "I've got to get out of here!" and with her help I turned and staggered out of the church. Once outside my symptoms rapidly subsided as I said, "Sorry, Sweetheart, I can't get married in there."

Ella's parents happened to be good friends with their local suburban Mayor, and the next evening Ella and I were married by the Mayor in his own residence in Lyndhurst, Ohio, I in my lieutenant's uniform and Ella, beautiful and shapely in her light golden dress. The ceremony was attended by Ella's sister, Helen, and my best friend, Dr. Phillip Perloff, my classmate in medical school and roommate at Fort Sam Houston, now serving as "best man." Although once again I experienced some anxiety, I was able to survive the brief ceremony. It saddened me to learn that my mother had forbidden any of my siblings from attending or supporting my heretical marriage, but I was pleased when two of my brothers came secretly to our post-ceremony celebration at Ella's family home. I realized that my anxiety attacks were due to my distress over my mother's religious condemnation.

The following morning, however, I was thrilled to receive a phone call from my mother, phoning us at the Cleveland downtown hotel where we spent our wedding night and were now waiting for our later departure by train to San Francisco. To my surprise, Mother urged that we come to her home to receive her blessing for our marriage! It appeared that she had experienced some sort of epiphany. At her home she explained that seren-dipitously she had received a phone call that very morning from a close friend who was a devout Catholic mother who was tearfully distraught about learning that her Catholic son had just announced his intent to marry his Protestant girlfriend. My mother, a natural born thera-pist, assured her friend that what really counted in her son's life was that he and his girlfriend loved each other, and not that they had different religious faiths.

As my mother heard her own voice comforting her friend, she realized the inconsistency of her own objection to my marriage, and at her conversation's end, she phoned for Ella and me to come for her blessing before we left for San Francisco. Ella, much hurt by my mother's protest over our marriage, reluctantly agreed to go with me in the spirit of reconciliation. I was happy for us to receive the hugs and kisses and good wishes from my family.

The next day we arrived by overnight train to San Francisco. We were disappointed to learn there would be a long waiting period of uncertain length for Ella to join me in Japan. After a few days of Army indoctrination I was waving good-bye to my bride from the deck of a military troop ship heading for the Pacific for its week-long voyage to Japan. When the ship arrived and docked at the Tokyo Bay harbor, I could see the war-strewn devastation of the city, not yet recovered from the many weeks of air raids and fire bombing it had endured during the war.

The shipload of army doctors disembarked and we were whisked away by train to an army post on the outskirts of the city. There we lived in tents while being interviewed by senior officers, given our assignments and briefed as to our impending duties. I expected to be assigned to an army hospital somewhere in Japan, but once again I experienced the fickle and mindless nature of military command. For no reason that had any bearing on my past medical experience or training, I was told to serve as the single Public Health Officer for the Port of Yokohama. I was provided with an office at the harbor with a sergeant to keep records as well as a small motor boat to take me to inspect every commercial ship seeking permission to dock at Yokohama Port. The motor boat would bring me alongside each freighter which always appeared to be huge, black and foreboding. A twenty-foot-long rope ladder would be tossed from the deck to the motor boat. Then with heart pounding, pulse racing and face sweating, I would have to climb up the swaying rope ladder until I was near enough to be reached by sailors on the ship who would then haul me aboard the deck.

The usual routine was that I would be heartily greeted by the captain of the ship, who would escort me to his private cabin, sit me down, bring out a bottle of red wine, toast me in whatever foreign language he usually toasted in, and then would regale me in English with stories of his lifetime travels. He would always assure me that none of

the crew on his ship were ill, none of his previous ports of
call had epidemic diseases, and that no rats were on
board. During the first few weeks of my serving as
Yokohama Port Officer, despite the captains' assurances,
I conscientiously examined all the medical records of the
crew and searched for rat droppings in the holds of their
ship before I cleared the ship for entry into the port. But
after a few weeks, as none of my inspections ever found
any evidence for denying the ship's entry, I simply accepted the captains' assurances and enjoyed their wine-
driven hospitality until enough time elapsed for me to
phone my sergeant that the "inspection" was over and the
ship was cleared for entry into Yokohama Port.

As a married lieutenant waiting for my wife to join me
in Japan, I was housed in bachelor officers' quarters in
Yokohama. I slept in a large room with about twenty-five
officers whose snoring, coughing and assorted noises kept
me awake most of each night. I recall vividly being awakened by one officer crawling along the floor beating
imaginary spiders with his shoe while shouting, "Out, you
damn spiders!" He was diagnosed with "Delirium Tre-
mens (DTs)" and was carted off to a military hospital for
treatment of his alcoholism.

After two months of duty as a port officer I was notified
that my wife was still on a waiting list that might take up
to ten more months. However, I was told that if I would
volunteer for the Paratroops Division stationed in Hok-
kaido, the northern island of Japan, she would be immediately brought to Japan. Torn between yearning for my
wife versus my deathly fear of having to jump out of
planes, I sent her a telegram stating that if she wanted, I
would indeed join the Paratroops. With much trepidation
I waited for her reply, and with much relief received her

answer that she did not wish to be married to a physician who had to jump out of a plane once a month.

After nine months as Port Officer I was promoted to rank of Captain and reassigned as Public Health Officer for the Prefecture of Fukuoka in Kyushu, the southern island of Japan. I was happy to be informed that my wife would arrive in Japan that month. After joyously greeting her when she did arrive at Yokohama, we traveled by train to Kurume, a small town in Kyushu, about a half-hour train ride from Fukuoka City, the capital of Fukuoka Prefecture (state), where the offices of the Fukuoka Military Government Team were located. In Kurume we were housed temporarily at "Suimei-so" (Clear Water Mansion), a magnificent Japanese estate with multiple rooms which were used by the Army both as Bachelor Officers Quarters and also for newly arrived army couples who would live there until the Army could "requisition" a suitable house for them in Fukuoka City. Suimei-so was an opulent, two-story mansion with a rolling green landscaped lawn surrounded by trees and flower beds and a large pond with birds and goldfish.

Since there were neither bachelor officers nor other couples staying there at that time, Ella and I lived there for two months, alone with thirteen Japanese house servants. We learned that this estate was the favorite of the fourteen homes owned by Mr. Ishibashi, one of the directors of the rubber industry of Japan. Apparently, in Japan at that time, each separate Japanese industry was owned for generations by a single family, the Zaibatsu system of industrial and financial corporations. Mr. Ishibashi's chauffeur-driven limousine drove up to the house a few days after Ella and I arrived, and I went out to greet him as he emerged from his car, an elderly, well-dressed

Japanese gentleman who spoke in clear English. "Welcome, Captain Fierman, is everything satisfactory for you and your wife in my house?"

Standing face-to-face with this wealthy, aristocratic Japanese tycoon, I sensed a hint of condescension in his soft-spoken inquiry. Was I looking at the face of the industrial component of the military-industrial complex of fascist Japan that had promulgated the bloody war against my country? I felt a growing anger and wanted to express it in some way. It occurred to me that Ella enjoyed playing the piano and so I responded, "Yes, Mr. Ishibashi, your house is magnificent, except that there is no piano for my wife."

"I will take care of that," he said impassively, bowed and drove away. The next day, a truck arrived and an elegant black grand piano was carted into the house. We lived in this idyllic setting for two months. A jeep with driver had been assigned to the house and he would drive me each weekday morning to a train station nearby where a Japanese train would stop and wait to take me to Fukuoka City, thirty miles away. The train had several cars, each extremely crowded with Japanese commuters, except for a single car reserved for Army personnel and marked with a wide red, white and blue stripe. Dressed in my captain's uniform, I was the solitary passenger in this train car. From my seat I could see the crowded passengers in the car ahead, some of them hanging precariously on the banisters of the steps into their car.

On one occasion as the train entered the station in Fukuoka City, it stopped suddenly. Checking the car door to see what was holding up the train, I could see a Japanese passenger had fallen off the steps of the car ahead and was lying motionless on the train tracks. To my horror I noticed several Japanese station personnel drag-

ging the unconscious man over the tracks by his ankles to
clear the way for the train! Jumping out of my car I ran to
the scene and stopped the dragging. Examining the man I
found he was alive but unconscious and had a bleeding
head injury. I gestured to the men watching that a
stretcher was needed, and to my surprise, several ran to
the office nearest the tracks, forcibly tearing down the
door to use as an emergency stretcher. Running back to
the unconscious passenger, they lifted him onto the door
and carried him off the tracks. One stayed behind to ask,
in broken English, my name and duties in Fukuoka City. A
few days after the incident, a Japanese man appeared at
my Fukuoka office who turned out to be the man I had
rescued. He thanked me profusely in Japanese through
my interpreter and brought a Japanese newspaper de-
scribing me as a heroic American Officer who had saved
his life.

My duties as Public Health Officer of the U.S. Military
Government Team for Fukuoka Prefecture were to assess
the health problems of the people in the Prefecture, supervise the Prefectural Health Department and its Director,
Doctor Sugino, inspect the Japanese hospitals, develop a
Health Center in Fukuoka and report all my activities
monthly to the Team Commander, Colonel Springer, and
also to the Tokyo headquarters of Colonel Crawford F.
Sams, Chief of the Public Health and Welfare Section of
the Supreme Command for the Allied Powers (SCAP) in
East Asia.

I was known to the Japanese as Tai-i san, Oisha-san,
Fierman-san (Captain Doctor Fierman). I had an office in
military government team headquarters in Fukuoka City,
a full-time Japanese interpreter, Dr. Ichiro Tokuyama, a
jeep and a driver. I was stationed there for the duration of
my uninterrupted two-year military service in Japan. I

enjoyed my work and was proud of my country for its magnanimous altruistic programs for rehabilitating our defeated former enemy. My only regret was that my duties were totally administrative and consultative and constituted a two-year lapse from my continuing clinical and medical training and development as a physician.

Socially I related mainly to Japanese citizens and health professionals and had very few contacts with American officers or soldiers. I did have close relationships with other American members of the Military Government Team and also with my interpreter and his wife, a journalist. Meanwhile, Ella obtained a job as elementary school teacher at the nearby U.S. Army Dependents School. She traveled with me on some of my trips and we did have off-time visits to tour the area, including Mt. Aso, a dormant volcano in southern Fukuoka, and we visited the ancient temples and the Emperor's summer palace in Kyoto.

I wired my mother back in Cleveland to send me my textbook on public health to help with my lectures. Ironically, in medical school public health was my least attended course and I had little interest then in the subject. But Japan was rife with serious public health problems. A high percentage of Japanese suffered from malnutrition, parasites like ascaris and hookworm contracted in their rice paddies, tuberculosis, polluted water, outbreaks of viral encephalitis and venereal disease. Prostitution had been legal in Japan before the Occupation, but General Douglas MacArthur declared it to be illegal as part of his reformation of Japan by fiat.

My work was interesting with much traveling with my interpreter, inspecting and lecturing on public health at health and medical facilities and Japanese civic organizations throughout the state of Fukuoka. My Japanese jeep driver and my interpreter tried to get me to sit in the back seat because they insisted the back seat was for "superior" persons. I refused and always sat in the front seat. In my lectures I would frequently include harsh condemnation of the pre-war totalitarian Japanese government for neglecting the public health of the country. On one occasion, however, an Australian missionary nun who was in the audience came up to me after the lecture and said, "Captain Fierman, that was a fine lecture, but unfortunately your interpreter did not say in Japanese what you said in English!" I angrily confronted my interpreter, Dr. Tokuyama, who responded plaintively by saying, "But, Dr. Fierman, you don't really want me to tell those people how bad their country was before, do you? It would only make them feel very bad." Although I sternly reprimanded him and insisted that in the future he must translate all my public statements fully and truthfully, I realized he was encouraging me to better understand the Japanese cultural avoidance of communicating negative, critical statements directly on any subject.

Dr. Tokuyama was an interesting man, and he and his wife and Ella and I became friends. He was my age, thirty-five, and had graduated from the Kyushu Imperial University School of Medicine in Fukuoka City and was trained in Internal Medicine. He had served as a navy medical officer on a Japanese destroyer during the war. He told me that when his ship was at sea the Japanese on board could listen in on American radio broadcasts reporting the devastating firebombing of Japan, while back in Japan, people could only receive Japanese broadcasts assuring them that Japan was winning the war. The commander of Dr. Tokuyama's ship became suicidally depressed after hearing that his family's home city was in flames and Dr. Tokuyama was ordered to treat him. He had received minimal training in psychiatry in his medical school, but he did have access to medical books on board and was able to read about electro-convulsive shock therapy for depression. Fortunately, the ship's pharmacy included a shock machine and he then recommended shock therapy for his commander. To his dismay, the commander consented to the treatment but only if Dr. Tokuyama himself would first submit to a shock treatment. Dr. Tokuyama agreed, and to my knowledge, is the only doctor who ever had himself shocked in order to demonstrate its safety. The course of shock treatments was successful and Tokuyama and his commander completed their sea duty and survived the war. Several years after the war Dr. Tokuyama and his wife toured the United States and visited Ella and me in Connecticut. Then, five years after his visit we were saddened to hear from his wife in Japan that Dr. Tokuyama had been killed by a stroke of lightning while playing golf on a rainy day.

My public health work also involved inspecting Japanese national hospitals which were either tuberculosis (TB) or mental hospitals. At that time general medical hospitals were owned by private physicians and functioned as small private clinics, each with operating rooms and beds. I found the national hospitals to be in dismal repair and short of nurses and doctors. There were no central kitchens, and food and personal nursing care had to be provided to patients by their own families. Starvation was a major cause of death in the national hospitals. Surgeons had no rubber gloves and had to use cotton gloves instead. Heat and cooking were provided by portable charcoal stoves brought in by patients' families.

Usually a relative would sleep on the floor next to the patient to provide for their needs as best they could. Surgical thoracoplasty (surgically collapsing the chest wall over the diseased lobe) was the treatment of choice in the TB hospitals because patients did not want to stay hospitalized for long, less drastic inpatient treatment with bed rest and medication. Mental hospitals were also in disarray with psychotic patients frequently caged, noisy, heavily sedated and poorly fed. Medical care was outdated and based on obsolete German practices. The first penicillin plant in Japan was built by the USA under the guidance of Dr. Jackson W. Foster who was invited to Japan by Colonel Sams.

General MacArthur had imperiously given women the right to vote, and he also ordered all institutions and businesses in Japan to permit the organization of unions for their employees. His order was largely misinterpreted as including hospital patients as well as hospital employees. As a result patients organized "patient unions" in national hospitals and they demanded special services, special meals, prostitutes for the patients, and funds for patients to attend patient union conventions in Tokyo and Yokohama. After I and other Military Government Public Health Officers throughout Japan reported this preposterous state of affairs to SCAP in Tokyo, the order was rescinded.

I also inspected the Kyushu University Medical School in Fukuoka City, where two years before my arrival in Japan in 1947, several Japanese doctors and nurses had been tried, convicted and executed by the Military Government for conducting lethal experiments on American prisoners in Japan's search for a blood substitute. I saw demonstrations of acupuncture therapy for various orthopedic disorders and I also urged the clinical staff to provide more humane care for the animals they used for research.

On another occasion, I was disgusted by reports that the Army Military Police in Fukuoka City, trying to prevent the spread of venereal disease among American troops, were seizing Japanese women who happened to be outside after dark on the assumption that they were prostitutes. The military police shaved off the women's hair as punishment and then took them to Japanese clinics for examination. When this was mistakenly done to a Japanese nun one night, I finally reported the entire practice by our military police to Colonel Sams in Tokyo and subsequently the practice was stopped by orders from SCAP.

Later I was invited to attend a conference of Military Government Public Health Officers and Japanese health officials in Fukuoka to discuss the promotion of contraception in Japan. It was hoped this would ease the problem of overpopulation, a problem that was a causative factor in Japan's military efforts to obtain more territory for its people. Japanese officials protested and claimed such a program would "weaken the moral fiber of the Nation." The proposal was scrapped.

My two years of duty as a Military Government Public Health Officer were lively and interesting and a gratifying personal experience, but perhaps the most profound and moving experience was my visit to Nagasaki to observe the devastation there and to meet some of the survivors of our country's dreadful nuclear bombing of that historic city.[1] In January of 1948, Captain Bill Dickerson, a fellow

---

[1] To view my letter and pictures of my visit to Nagasaki, see Appendix 4. p. 161ff.

military government public health officer and my Japanese interpreter, Dr. Ichiro Tokuyama, met with me in Fukuoka, Japan. We piled into an army jeep and drove the 150 miles to meet Captain Elliot, the public health officer in Nagasaki. We had met previously to arrange this trip to visit Nagasaki, the small seaport fishing village which was the second city after Hiroshima to be devastated by a single atomic bomb dropped by order of President Truman on August 9, 1945. This was to force Japan to surrender, ending the war with us. The bomb exploded in midair about a thousand feet above ground, flattening most of the buildings located in the valley just outside the city, setting fire to all paper and wooden houses and structures in the city. Approximately twenty thousand Japanese were killed instantly and another sixty thousand died within a year from radiation and burn injuries.

Ironically, Nagasaki was predominantly the only Catholic Japanese city, since early European ships from Spain and Portugal landed there to trade with Japan. These ships usually carried priests who were successful in converting many Japanese who were involved with international commercial trading. The single Catholic church, located in the center of the valley, was leveled by the bomb blast except for its front wall which remained standing. The church's priest, Father Monfetti, a French-Canadian, had been interned by the Japanese military throughout the war. He met us at the church site and served as our guide and interpreter. He had arranged for six men and women who survived the bomb blast to meet and speak with us. They were all simple farm folks who had been working in the fields at the periphery of the valley when the bomb exploded about a half mile distant from them. They showed us their thick, pink "keloid" scars on their arms, faces and necks caused by the intense radiation of

the atomic bomb. Strangely, their clothing seemed to have
protected the rest of their bodies. Father Monfetti reported that these survivors happened to be outside their
homes when the bomb exploded. Their families, indoors
at the time, were all killed by the instant conflagration of
their houses. As the Japanese survivors spoke to us
through their priest interpreter, their voices were soft
spoken, without bitterness or rancor. I was overwhelmed
by the plight of these innocent civilian survivors and the
devastation of their city and I asked the priest to extend
my deepest regret and sympathy. They were silent, down-
cast and impassive. Father Monfetti then suggested,
"Please ask them how they feel about the United States
dropping a nuclear bomb on their peaceful, fishing and
farming village." I did and after a long pause, one farmer
replied softly in Japanese. The priest interpreted, "He says
it was not a gentlemanly thing to do!"

We thanked them all and left, shaken, silent and very
sad. Any thoughts that I ever had that the bombing was
necessary and justified to end the war and prevent continuing loss of American casualties were overcome by
witnessing the terror and devastation wreaked on an
innocent civilian fishing village, much worse than any use
of universally condemned poison gas.

In July of 1949, my two years of active military service
came to an end and Ella and I said farewell to our Military
Government colleagues and all our Japanese friends in
Fukuoka. I had applied and had been accepted by the Yale
University School of Medicine for a residency in Internal
Medicine held at the Veterans Administration Hospital in
Newington, Connecticut.

In Tokyo, as Ella and I waited to board the military
ship that would take us home, we reflected on our life in
Japan. We had been exposed to a culture vastly different

from our American background, a culture much older than ours, steeped in Buddhist ethos rather than Judeo-Christian beliefs. We had been part of a historic occupation of a country and nation defeated in a long and bloody war, cities devastated by widespread fire bombing and a final war-ending catastrophic nuclear bombing of helpless civilians in two Japanese cities. Yet, due to the amazing ability of General MacArthur and Emperor Hirohito to assure the Japanese people that they would be treated humanely and would be helped to become rehabilitated and healed as a nation, we Americans were accepted and respected with gratitude and friendship by the Japanese. Ella and I realized that there had been no fear of danger throughout our stay, and without exception, all the Japanese we met or worked with were extremely friendly to us.

5

"FOR GOD, COUNTRY AND YALE"

5

"FOR GOD, COUNTRY AND YALE"

"All aboard!" The call came from the deck of the Navy troop ship ready to transport over one hundred army medical officers and wives from Tokyo, Japan to Seattle, Washington. It was June, 1949. I had completed my required two years of active military service as Military Government Public Health Officer during the post WWII occupation of Japan. Ella and I enjoyed the five-day ocean voyage playing day-long bridge games with fellow officers and their wives. We were thrilled at our first sighting of the magnificent American coastline and, in the distance, the snow-capped peak of Mt. Rainier. After landing in Seattle I declined the invitation of the Army Medical Corps to extend my enlistment and, as a civilian once more, I and Ella began our four-day cross-country drive to our families in Cleveland and Lyndhurst, Ohio.

In Japan I had misgivings that my two-year absence from clinical medicine would put me at a disadvantage competing against recent medical school graduates for residency training appointments. As a precaution I applied to five different training institutions in the U.S.A. and was pleased to be accepted by all of them. I picked Yale's residency program in Internal Medicine because of Yale's prestige and because the starting salary was $3600 per annum. In the 1940s most residency programs offered only room and board with little or no salaries. I thought that with Yale's salary plus our meager Army savings we would be able to manage financially during my residencies, while Ella pursued her doctoral studies in psychology at Yale.

Our drive through the countryside of the USA gave us new appreciation of the grandeur and opulence of our homeland compared to war-torn Japan. In Ohio we were greeted warmly by our families and Ella remained there while I continued on to Connecticut to check in at the hospital and establish our living quarters.

The Yale residency program in Internal Medicine was offered in the Veterans Administration Hospital in Newington, Connecticut. At the hospital I reported to the chief of medicine. He welcomed me, briefed me on my duties and then assigned a temporary room for me to share overnight with another veteran, Martin Gordon, M.D. I met Gordon that evening and to my dismay he shocked me with the question, "Isn't it a shame about our salaries?"

"What shame? What salaries?"

"Our salaries. They claim they've made a mistake. The salary is $1800 instead of $3600."

After a sleepless night I was able to confront the Chief the next morning with my written notice of acceptance with a salary of $3600 that had been sent to me in Japan.

"Look, Fierman," he said, "sorry about the mistake, but if you make a fuss about this, you'll be blackballed in every hospital in the country. If you need more money, why doesn't your wife get a job?"

"My wife is applying to graduate school and I won't ask her to give that up just because you won't pay enough for us to live on."

"Fierman," he countered, "you shouldn't have gotten married in the first place until you were through with your residencies." Angrily I told him I had to return to Cleveland to consult with Ella as to whether I should accept the residency at reduced pay or go directly into private practice as a general practitioner. He agreed that I could take the week off to decide.

When I arrived back in Ohio, Ella urged me to take the residency and said she would get a job in Connecticut to supplement our income, putting off her doctoral studies until I had completed my training. I began my residency in internal medicine while Ella found work as a psychologist at Hartford Hospital. The VA hospital offered us living quarters in a military Quonset hut on hospital grounds, but we found comparable facilities nearby.

My patient care duties on the medical wards required that I be on call every other night and every other weekend. As I had predicted in Japan, I found that my two-year absence from clinical medicine put my job performance well behind the other residents who were more advanced and knowledgeable about clinical medical terms and practices. It soon became clear to me that my chief regarded me as a dunce, and my standing with him was further strained when my wife informed me she had rejected his flirtatious overtures, consistent with his reputation, during social gatherings for residents and their wives.

The residency was a three-year pyramidal program, meaning that fewer residents were appointed for the second year and fewer again for the third and final year of training. I became resigned to the expectation that after my first year I probably would not be kept on staff and I would have to find another hospital for continued training. But the medical residency did involve a one month's rotation through the psychiatric service of the hospital. To my surprise, I enjoyed the work with psychiatric patients even more than I did with patients on the medical wards. On the medical service I had been criticized for spending too much time talking with my patients, but on psychiatry, I was praised by the senior staff for my ability to establish therapeutic relationships with patients. "You're a natural therapist," one of them declared and urged me to switch from internal medicine to psychiatry. Ella was also enthusiastic about the idea, even though it meant adding three more years of residency training in psychiatry to my one year in medicine. The final inducement was when she expressed her hope that if I specialized in psychiatry we could be in joint practice together.

With these hopes and with much trepidation about my future I requested a transfer from internal medicine to psychiatry and was accepted. When I phoned my parents in Cleveland to tell them of my switch to psychiatry, my father asked, "Are you sure you want to be a crazy doctor?" My mother's response to me was, "But can you still write a prescription?" Despite their limited knowledge about psychiatry they both gave me their heartfelt wishes for my success.

In July of 1950 I began my first year of Yale's residency program in psychiatry at the Newington, Connecticut VA Hospital, but in the first week I had to travel to New Haven to attend an orientation meeting for new residents held by Frederick C. Redlich, M.D., Chairman of the Yale Depart-

ment of Psychiatry. He was a robust forty-year-old professor who spoke with a slight German accent. He welcomed
us to the Department and closed his remarks with a stern
warning, "Gentlemen, this is a psychoanalytic department and if you want to stay, I advise you to beg, borrow
or steal the money and begin your own analysis."

The hourly fee for psychoanalysis then was fifty dollars and therapy sessions were held four times a week. The
annual cost would be about ten thousand dollars and I
had no way of raising such a sum. I read in a psychoanalytic journal that some senior analysts accepted IOUs
from students for payment to be paid after completion of
the student's residency. I made the rounds of analysts in
the New Haven area seeking such an arrangement, but
none of them proved willing. One elderly female analyst
explained that such an arrangement would compromise
the analysis because it "would muffle the transference."
My promise to not muffle anything did not dissuade her. I
had to postpone my analysis until completion of my residency.

The residency years were replete with dramatic, challenging patients to treat, and distinguished faculty supervisors sharing their expertise. In addition, there was a vast
amount of professional literature in medicine, neurology,
psychology and psychoanalysis to master. I was taught
then that the core basic identity of a psychiatrist was to be
a psychotherapist, and that long-term psychoanalysis was
the ideal definitive, curative, and transformational
therapy for psychoneurotic patients. However, since we
residents were neither qualified nor trained to provide
psychoanalysis, we were trained instead to offer, as a
second choice, a watered-down, condensed version of
psychoanalysis; namely, short-term, psychoanalytically-

oriented psychotherapy. We were taught that a proviso for a patient to qualify for either version of psychoanalytic therapy was that he had to be intelligent, motivated, psychologically sophisticated and neurologically intact. For the many patients who did not meet these requirements, supportive psychotherapy was provided instead. Of course, none of these attitudes, conditions or practices were evidence-based truisms, but rather they were unproven beliefs and convictions that evolved along with the psychoanalytic movement started by Sigmund Freud, and, unfortunately, are maintained to this day by the psychoanalytic community despite their lack of validity (Fierman, 1965).

In my Yale psychiatric residency, 1950 to 1953, I accepted and believed uncritically all these psychoanalytic beliefs and principles, and had every intention of becoming a psychoanalyst myself. In my third year I was appointed by Dr. Redlich as Chief Resident for both the Yale Psychiatric Institute and also the Yale-New Haven Hospital Psychiatric Service. To supplement my meager Yale salary I rented an office for evening use at one dollar per hour and began a "moonlight" evening private practice of psychotherapy. Meanwhile, Ella was hired at Yale as a psychology research assistant.

In July of 1953, my residency training was completed and I accepted an offer from Dr. Redlich to join the psychiatric faculty as an Assistant Clinical Professor. He appointed me to be chief of a ward for chronically ill, chronically hospitalized, elderly male schizophrenic veterans at the Veterans Administration Hospital in West Haven, Connecticut. Such patients usually had long histories of failed therapies and were now housed for life in so-called "back wards" of mental hospitals, medicated to subdue any agitation or potential violence and living out their days as passive, incoherent, zombie-like automatons.

I was not willing simply to accept their being written off as hopeless and not suitable for any continued therapy other than compassionate nursing care, yet formal psychotherapy seemed out of the question with these aging demented patients, and I had no staff other than a few ward nurses and nurses' aides. I was familiar with innovative work done by Dr. Maxwell Jones in England and described in his book *The Therapeutic Community* (1953). He had been successful in rehabilitating chronic neurotic veterans by treating them in a facility where every member of both the clinical and administrative staff, including kitchen and maintenance employees, were designated as "therapists" and were directed to meet, speak and interact with the patients individually and in groups. I decided to establish a similar "therapeutic community" on my ward. To do this, I directed all the ward nurses and nurses' aides to relate to the patients as psychotherapists under my supervision. There were initial protests from the staff, complaints that the patients were unresponsive, frequently mute and inaccessible, but I encouraged them to persist as group therapists and divided their patients into groups of six patients per group.

After a few days I was directed to report to the office of the chief of the psychiatry service, Eugene B. Brody, M.D., where I was angrily confronted by the Director of Psychiatric Nursing, who complained bitterly that I had usurped her authority by directing her ward nursing personnel to be group therapists under my supervision. Dr. Brody listened to her attack, then tersely told her that he agreed with me and with my use of her staff. After she stormed out of his office, he reprimanded me for not having tried to get her cooperation prior to beginning my project. She later transferred to another hospital. It felt good to know I had the support of my chief, but I was sad that I had alienated the nursing director.

A turning point on the ward occurred a few weeks afterward when one of the nurses' aides went on sick leave and his group therapy was temporarily suspended. To the staff's surprise his group of patients who had previously been essentially mute and unresponsive, showed up daily at the nurses' station to ask plaintively when their therapist would return. When he finally did reappear, the group was openly pleased and his sessions with them became more lively and interactive. I felt my project had been vindicated and that significant behavioral change in chronic demented patients could be achieved by a therapist offering a sustained friendly, supportive, communicative relationship, even though the therapist was not trained to provide psychoanalytically-oriented therapy.

Now that I had salaried employment, I could pursue my wish to become a psychoanalyst. I applied for admission to the Western New England Psychoanalytic Institute and was subjected to interviews and psychological tests. I was then advised that their limited number of acceptances for 1953 had been filled, but that I should begin my personal analysis now and reapply the following year for admission to the Institute. I agreed and searched for a psychoanalyst, but none of the New Haven analysts had openings in their practice. However, I was informed that Hellmuth Kaiser, Ph.D., a training analyst from the Menninger Psychoanalytic Institute in Topeka, Kansas had moved to West Hartford and was now accepting new patients. I phoned and he scheduled four hourly sessions per week at a fee reduced to $20.00 per hour in view of my limited income.

Dr. Kaiser was a sixty-year-old, balding, sad-looking, trim-built man, wearing a tan wool cardigan sweater. He spoke to me in his waiting room with a mild German accent, "Dr. Fierman? Please come in." I entered his office and went directly to the office couch and reclined on it, certain that I was following the appropriate protocol for a beginning analysand. He sat silently in a lounge chair not entirely behind the head of the couch where I assumed, since Freud, a psychoanalyst was supposed to sit. *He's not sitting in the right place*, I thought, *maybe it's because he seems so old and casual.* To conform to what I thought was the "correct" psychoanalytic position for an analysand, I shifted to my right side so that my back was towards Kaiser, and I could not see him while I "free associated" (psychoanalytic jargon for reporting everything that comes to mind, no matter how much one's thoughts were disconnected or rambling.)

Without further ado, I launched into a narrative review of the circumstances that led to my phoning him to arrange for an analysis. When I paused he commented, "So it's not that you wanted to be treated or helped to change in any way?" "Well, no," I stammered, "I don't claim to be perfectly healthy, but I didn't think I needed therapy. I just want to do whatever it is I need to do to become a psychoanalyst." He was silent while I continued with my narrative until he finally said, "We have to stop now." I stood up and left.

Weeks passed as I continued with my monologue, sharing my random thoughts no matter how bizarre. Kaiser commented infrequently with cryptic remarks, such as, "You remind me of a chicken laying an egg."

"What? Why?" I asked.

"A chicken seems indifferent and unconcerned before, during or after her egg plops out. You seem to have a slide in your head where any thought that occurs in your mind mindlessly slides down and plops out of your mouth."

"But that's "free association," isn't it?" I said, "and that's what I'm supposed to be doing here, isn't it?"

"Who says?" he asked and then relapsed into his usual silence.

That exchange led to my giving up mindless reporting and instead I began reporting the ups and downs of my daily life at home and at work, both in the present and in the past. I noticed that I had become eager to go to each session, and sorry for each session to end. It felt good to share my past and present life with this gentle, attentive nonjudgmental listener.

The year passed quickly, and as directed by the Institute the year before, I reapplied for admission. Once again there were interviews and psychological tests, and then I was advised that since I appeared to be much improved psychologically since beginning my analysis, they urged that I first complete my personal analysis and then reapply for admission to the Institute. Since I had already paid the application fee twice, there would be no fee for my third application.

Paradoxically, I became aware in my continued analysis with Dr. Kaiser that, rather than being annoyed with the delaying tactics received from the Institute faculty, I was actually relieved by their decision and had growing doubts as to whether I should become a psychoanalyst. In my sessions with Dr. Kaiser I began to complain and ridicule the procedure itself. "It's silly to lie on this couch and talk without looking at you."

"Yes, isn't it," he responded.

"Then why do you analysts want your patients to do that?"

"Well, it's not that I want you not to do that, but it is not so that I want you to do that."

"But am I not supposed to lie down and free associate?"

"Who says?"

I sat up angry, faced him and shouted, "Then why do you have this couch here if you don't want me to lie on it!"

"I use it to take a nap whenever I feel tired."

That interaction affected me profoundly. My therapy became face-to-face. Kaiser's sole activity throughout my therapy was to accept me unconditionally and nonjudgmentally and to share with me his thoughts and feelings about my verbal and nonverbal behavior with him. I realized that my relationship with Kaiser had become my therapy, not my undergoing some sort of analytic experience. He had obviously defected from psychoanalytic orthodoxy and instead was offering me an intensely personal, nondirective and egalitarian relationship.[1] Without the subjects being addressed or discussed I noticed that various symptoms I had throughout my adult life had disappeared; namely, anxiety, migraine headaches and palpitations whenever I had to speak with a superior. Also, my psychotherapy with patients had become more effective as I adopted Dr. Kaiser's nondirective and communicative sharing attitude with them.

My therapy lasted three years, 1953 to 1956, after which I reapplied to the Psychoanalytic Institute. In my interview, the training analyst became annoyed on hearing that I no longer wished to be a practicing psycho-

---

[1] For more on Dr. Kaiser's becoming a nondirective psychotherapist, see Appendix 1, p. 115.

analyst, but still regarded psychoanalytic training as useful and informative for my work as a Kaiserian psychotherapist. He arrogantly rejected my application saying,
"That's like being an electrician applying for training in
nuclear physics!"

At age thirty-four, in 1956, my life changed dramati-
cally. I ended my therapy with Dr. Kaiser after three
years, gave up my goal of becoming a psychoanalyst,
replacing it by becoming a Kaiserian, nondirective, communicative-intimacy therapist, and, most surprising, I
was informed by Ella that within nine months or so I
would become a father!

When we had married just before I went to Japan, Ella
had stipulated that she wanted to pursue her career as a
research psychologist and did not want to have children.
Although I wished very much for children, I conceded
that it was her right to decide when, where and if she
would consent. However, her objection to having children was more than balanced by her love of animals. But
love is not quite the right word for it . She *feels* intensely
for animals—all animals. I'm sure if I were some sort of
beast other than a human, it would have spared us many
of the squabbles that occasionally marred our otherwise
happy fifty-eight years of marriage. Ella was born a rural
suburban girl and her family had a cat or a dog all her life.
The first dog, a lively part Spitz, lived with her throughout
her childhood and finally died at age eighteen. That's
supposed to be equivalent to 126 human years. In contrast, I did not have any pets in my childhood or even like
animals for that matter. I was an inner-city boy and feared
the many roaming dogs that always seemed to threaten
me on my daily walk to elementary school.

After we married I soon became aware of the intensity
of her emotional attachment and concern about dogs,

cats, birds, butterflies, fish, whales, squirrels, rabbits—
you name it. I silently regarded her attitude towards
animals as rather childish but also found it somewhat
admirable and charming. She reminded me of the saintly
Doctor Schweitzer who allegedly would not light candles
in his quarters in the African jungle lest it would kill the
moths that flew into it at night.

Occasionally it became a nuisance that I felt obliged to
indulge. For instance, if while driving we should happen
to pass the dead body of some dog, cat or other varmint
lying in the street, a casualty of some preceding careless
or murderous driver, she would insist that we pull over to
the side of the road for me to get out of the car to retrieve
the carcass and move it off the road in order for it to
experience a more dignified disintegration back to the
dust to which all bodies eventually come, rather than for
it to remain in the street to be splattered about by the
traffic.

Our two children also loved animals and kept many
pets at home including gerbils, rabbits, cats and dogs. Our
daughter, Lauren, loved horses, took her horse with her
when she went off to college, and became a skillful winning competitive equestrienne. Over the years we owned
many fine dogs. In Japan we were given two dogs as
farewell gifts by Japanese health officials, one a pure bred
Akita, the other an Akita-Tosu crossbreed. Our son, Dan,
helped raise a Rhodesian Ridgeback and Lauren owned a
beagle. Our cats included three Himalayans and Ella
raised two turtles, originally tiny gifts to our kids but then
they grew to old and large turtle adulthood. For a time
each morning Ella went outdoors to place a bowl of food
for stray and neighboring cats. Then she filled numerous
bird feeders for the blue jays, cardinals and assorted
sparrows. Finally, food was scattered for the crows, squir-

rels, chipmunks, raccoons and wild turkeys that fre-
quented our front and back yards.

One day our daughter's girlfriend inadvertently released her pet mouse in our station wagon. From then on
Ella would place water and food for the mouse to feed
when it wasn't hiding in the nooks and crannies of the rest
of the wagon. Whenever she took the car to be serviced,
she would have to warn the workers not to be startled if
they saw a mouse in the car.

Of course, she vehemently opposed medical research
that involved harming animals, or movies and television
programs in which animals were injured or trained to
perform demeaning behavior. Circuses, rodeos and bull
fights were condemned and she abhorred the sight of
unhappy caged animals in a zoo. Through it all I humored
and indulged her, including sending donations to agen-
cies protecting animals: The Humane Society, Save the
Whales, Fund for Animals, etc.—you name it—we supported it. "How quaint of her," I used to say to myself,
"part of *her* loving character, but definitely not for *me*." I
would never go ga-ga over animals. The Bible says God
gave dominion over all the creatures of the Earth to Man,
and that includes me, and that means animals should
serve us and not the other way around.

But then something happened that changed everything and I became a Born Again Animal Lover. Our dog,
Lady, or I should say my wife's dog, Lady, suddenly
became ill. Lady was the beautiful ten-year-old Akita,
given to us as a puppy by Japanese friends while we were
both serving with the U.S. Army of Occupation in Japan.
We took Lady to a local veterinarian who said she required surgery to relieve an intestinal obstruction—no
problem—piece of cake. The operation was done and was
declared by the Vet to be a "success," but driving home

with Lady resting on my lap while Ella drove, Lady suddenly stopped breathing! We learned later that Lady had suffered a pulmonary embolism, but in the car I panicked and desperately attempted artificial respiration. We sped back to the Vet, but to no avail. Lady was dead and gone! Tenderly I carried Lady out to our backyard and teary-eyed, we buried her with full honors in our pet cemetery. That night I woke suddenly from a fitful sleep. Glaring light was streaming through our open bedroom doorway. Bathed in golden light, framed in the doorway was *my* dog, Lady! Ears perked, bushy tail curled, tan-colored hair glowing, panting and waiting eagerly for me to call her for fun, games and nuzzling. "Lady!" I shouted aloud, sitting upright in my bed, my heart full of love for my pet, my arms outstretched. "Lady!" I called, but slowly, ever so slowly, Lady gradually faded away and was gone! No lights—no open door—no loving and loved pet. The weird experience seemed to have broken through the animal barrier in my mind and heart. I missed Lady but now found all animals to be sentient and lovable creatures. I became a vegetarian, no longer comfortable about eating the bodies of harvested animals. I now oppose the frivolous and unnecessary use of animals for research, and I enthusiastically join my wife in doing everything we can to preserve, protect, respect and revere the creatures "large and small" that have survived the centuries and now precariously share our planet with us.

In our ninth year of marriage I was overjoyed when Ella resigned from her research activities at Yale and decided that we finally should have children. I eagerly agreed, but during her pregnancy felt I had to prepare to become a suitable playmate for our children and took lessons in swimming, ice skating and tennis. Ella opted for "natural" childbirth and on September 16, 1956, our son,

Daniel, was born, adorable, bald and looking very much like a miniature Eisenhower. Our second child, Lauren, a wonderful, frisky, beautiful little girl, was born three years later to complete our family. My father, who had died of heart failure at age sixty-five in 1952, never knew his grandchildren, but my mother enjoyed having them visit during our yearly trips to Cleveland, until her sudden death from a heart attack at age seventy in 1965. I deeply grieved the loss of both my parents who had provided me with unconditional love and support throughout my years with them.

I ended my therapy with Kaiser after three years because I felt the therapy had successfully "cured" me of my anxiety-related symptoms and had given me a new feeling of freedom and competence. I arranged with Kaiser for him to consult and supervise my clinical work. After completing my residency in 1953, I was appointed to the Yale faculty as an Assistant Clinical Professor in Psychiatry and as a Ward Chief on the Psychiatric Service of the Veterans Administration Hospital in West Haven, Connecticut. I met with Dr. Kaiser bi-weekly for his supervision of my evening private practice and also joined his weekly study group for his ex-patients, most of whom were either psychiatrists, psychologists or social work psychotherapists.

After word spread throughout the psychiatric and psychoanalytic community in Connecticut that he had defected from orthodox psychoanalysis, fewer patients were referred to him. He decided to accept an invitation from a former Menninger student to come and practice in California. In 1959 he left Connecticut and moved to Pacific Palisades, California where he lived, practiced and also wrote a monograph titled *The Universal Symptom of the Psychoneuroses: A Search for the Conditions of*

Effective Psychotherapy (Kaiser, 1959). Unfortunately, before he was able to find a publisher willing to publish his book, he died suddenly of a heart attack in 1961 at age 68. His widow, Ruth Kaiser, following his previous instructions in case of his death, mailed his manuscript to me and requested that I arrange for publication. She then left the country and returned to her native land of Israel with her teenage son. Kaiser's book, already rejected by nineteen publishers when I received it, was included as the main selection of an anthology of his writings that I edited and titled: *Effective Psychotherapy—The Contribution of Hellmuth Kaiser* (Fierman, ed., 1965). My book was then rejected by ten more publishers. I became aware of a pattern of rejection by the publishers. First, the book would be favorably reviewed by one of the junior editors of each firm who would then pass it on to the firm's consultant, usually a senior psychoanalyst, who would then condemn the book as heresy for taking issue with orthodox and traditional Freudian psychoanalysis. Finally, Robert R. Holt, Ph.D., a friend of Kaiser, persuaded his own publisher, The Free Press, to consider publishing the book. The Editor of Free Press wrote to me offering to publish the book on condition I send him $3000 on completion of the publication process to help cover costs. I promised to pay the sum but would need time to raise the money. He accepted my promise and the book was published in 1965. Since I personally did not have the money needed, I invited donations from my friends and Kaiser's relatives and colleagues. Twenty-five responded and I placed the $3000 in a local bank account, pending a call from the publisher. To my surprise no call came, and, instead, royalties were sent to me which I forwarded to Kaiser's widow in Israel. In 1967 the simmering warfare between Israel and the Palestine refugees flared up again, and Ruth Kaiser's letters indicated that the Israeli civilian population, including herself and her son, were enduring hardships. On a Friday I mailed the $3000 to Ruth Kaiser in Jerusalem, reasoning that apparently The Free Press no longer needed the money I had been saving for them. To my chagrin, the following Monday I received a letter from The Free Press requesting the money! I phoned the Editor and my explanation elicited laughter and assurance of no worry since the money would be retrieved from book sale royalties. The book received favorable reviews and sold over 4000 copies over a ten-year period before it went out of print.

Meanwhile, my career was flourishing. In 1961, Dr. Redlich notified me that the chief of psychiatry at the Veterans Administration Hospital was leaving and asked if I would like to be considered to succeed him as chief. After I said "Yes," a few days later he phoned telling me that his advisory committee of senior, tenured professors objected to my appointment as chief because I was not a psychoanalyst, and he felt obliged to comply with their choice of another member of the faculty who was an analyst. A few days later he phoned telling me he was appointing me to be chief after all. Later I learned that when he offered the promotion to the advisory committee's choice, the analyst agreed only on condition that his academic rank be raised from assistant professor to associate professor. Redlich refused and then appointed me over the objections of his advisory committee. Paradoxically, about a month later, he raised my rank to Associate Professor in Psychiatry.

I was chief from 1960 to 1970. The veterans on our wards received a full spectrum of individual and group psychotherapy, family therapy, psychopharmacotherapy and activities therapy. Clinical training for psychiatry residents and psychology interns and clerkships for Yale medical students were provided. Research and clinical articles were published. I was elected as President of the Connecticut Psychiatric Society and also attended seminars on Community Psychiatry at Duke University. My tenure as chief came to an end in 1970 when Dr. Redlich became Dean of the Yale School of Medicine and the new Chairman of the Yale Psychiatry Department replaced me with a psychoanalyst of his choice.

I had hoped for a lifetime academic career and was proud of my record as Chief of Psychiatry at the VA Hospital, but my displacement by the new Chairman was a narcissistic injury, meaning, it hurt my self-esteem. I then sadly decided to resign from full-time faculty and enter into full-time private practice with emphasis on Kaiserian psychotherapy.

6

THE LIFE AND DEATH
OF A HUMANISTIC
MENTAL HOSPITAL

6

THE LIFE AND DEATH OF A HUMANISTIC MENTAL HOSPITAL

My depressed mood over leaving full time Yale faculty in 1970 was accompanied by anxiety over entering full-time private practice in New Haven. A close friend of mine, Anthony Velonis, noted my distress and suggested as a diversion that I spend a weekend with him at his country house in Massachusetts to conduct an experiment with lysergic acid diethylamide (LSD). LSD was very much in the news at that time as a psychedelic drug that produced interesting euphoria but was also addictive and hallucinatory. It had become a cult-like drug with adherents claiming it opened the mind to new appreciation of cosmic spiritual reality and, in Europe, it was being used by a few psychiatrists as treatment for depression.

Tony Velonis, in his 60s, was an artist of repute who also owned an artist supplies factory in New Jersey. I had met him and his wife, Betty, at informal meetings I and Ella attended with friends who were interested in new developments in so-called humanistic psychology, including gestalt therapy, transcendentalism, bioenergetics, psychodrama and other esoteric practices, all on the fringe of mainstream psychology and psychiatry. Tony had a history of a car accident years before, which left him with a residual, traumatic back injury causing recurrent back pain of varying intensity. He discovered that a small dose of LSD would relieve his pain whenever it became severe, and he carried a small vial of LSD around his neck for such exigencies.

I accepted his invitation and Tony urged that Ella accompany me in order to drive home in case my driving was affected by the LSD experiment. I preferred that she not come since I knew she disapproved, but she assured me she would not interfere. At Tony's country home, there was a main house where Tony and Betty lived and a smaller log cabin house nearby for visitors. Tony shared with us that LSD had affected his understanding of life and appreciation of nature and was eager to introduce me to those new insights. He asked me for the name of my favorite composer (Tchaikovsky).

Saturday morning Ella and I arrived and after lunch Ella and Betty stayed in the large house while Tony and I descended to the smaller house. There he provided me with a fairly large oral dose of LSD while he took a small dose, explaining that would make him more available as my "guide" during the experiment. I noticed that on a table he had placed an array of flowers and fruit and a small screen for projecting slides. He turned on a record of Tchaikovsky music, the sound coming from two ceiling loudspeakers We chatted for about fifteen minutes when I began to feel a sense of increasing oppression. Although it was a bright sunny day, the room seemed to darken and everything around me began to become increasingly intense. The colors of the fruit and flowers became starkly intense and then the flowers began to pulsate! Tony projected some slides showing ancient temples with massive cobwebs and I was alarmed to feel the cobwebs in my mouth. I could see small bugs and insects crawling up and down the log cabin walls. Then the music became very loud and I stood up, faced the loudspeakers and shouted, "Tchaikovsky, you faggot! You sold out and composed schmaltz instead of real classical music!" Then, to my horror, standing across from me where Tony had just been standing before, was a devil! A huge, red-eyed, glaring, gigantic devil with horns and forked tail and claws extended towards me. Again I shouted, "I know you can kill me, but I won't go down easy!" To my amazement the giant devil gradually shrank in size and became Tony once more. "Lou," he said, "I'm not trying to kill you." But as soon as he stopped talking, he began to turn slowly back to his fierce devilish form. I suspected that the devil was waiting to attack me while I was looking at the display of pulsating flowers; I backed away from him to the corner of the room and curled up on the floor in a fetal position with eyes closed and ears covered. Tony changed the record to some Cage piano music. The sound was painful to my ears and I felt that I was being tortured. Tony stopped the music and said, "Let's go outside where I think you will feel better."

We walked outside and I could see everything pulsating—the grass, the trees and the leaves. I felt deeply depressed. There was a large pond ahead, and I thought to myself, "You shit! The only decent thing you can do is drown yourself in the pond!" I walked rapidly toward the pond with every intent of jumping in while Tony was behind me trying to keep up. Suddenly I heard the sound of Betty banging the iron triangle hanging in front of her door announcing that dinner was ready and Tony held my arm and guided me to the main house.

We four sat silent around the dinner table as Betty served soup. I looked at Ella and could see the skin of her face bleeding and curling. "You see! I told you not to come!" I shouted, but they just sat silent, not looking at me. Tony got up and got his fireplace poker to arrange the logs in his burning fireplace. I whispered to Ella and Betty, "He wants to kill me and after that he will kill you both!" I then noticed a mirror on the wall and went over to look at myself, To my surprise I could see my left pupil dilated and my right pupil constricted and all my senses and rationality were immediately restored. "I'm having a cerebral malfunction caused by LSD," I called out, much to the relief of the others there. Tony sadly explained that I had a "bad trip" which sometimes happens and urged that we try again some time. I agreed but it never happened. After assuring everyone that I was normal again, I suggested to Ella that we should retire to our cabin for the night. "I'm not going anywhere with you," Ella responded, but after more assurances from me she consented. That night I slept well and the next day we drove home. I had learned from my LSD hallucinatory and delusional experience that I had the potential to be psychotic, paranoid and suicidal and that there was a homicidal devil somewhere in the depths of my being.

Unfortunately, both my depression over leaving Yale and my anxiety over succeeding in private practice continued unabated. New Haven already had hundreds of psychiatrists, psychologists and social workers all competing in private practice. Would I ever get enough referrals to support my family? Within a month, to my great relief and gratitude, my friends and colleagues at Yale filled my practice hours with enough referrals that my income exceeded the combined salaries I had formerly received at Yale and the Veterans Administration Hospital.

Ella joined my practice as a psychotherapist and together we provided our patients with individual, couples, family and group psychotherapy. Several psychologist colleagues also joined our practice as did my friend and partner, Lane Ameen, M.D. We organized as Psychotherapy Associates, a mental health group practice in New Haven with me as Medical Director and Ella as Executive Director.

However, despite the success of our practice, my depressed mood over leaving Yale continued into the summer. Ella and I sent our two children to summer camp and, on our way to the 1970 annual meeting of the American Psychiatric Association in Los Angeles, we joined four colleagues and their wives in a week-long guided rafting trip down the Colorado River through the Grand Canyon. The trip was proposed by my close friend, Harvey R. Wasserman, M.D., a brilliant and charismatic psychiatrist, always open and willing to try new developments in alternative medicine and psychotherapy, including bioenergetics and gestalt therapies. Despite his busy practice in Westport, Connecticut, he and his wife, Rhoda, managed at least one annual exotic travel vacation. For our Grand Canyon trip he arranged for a large rubber raft to take us down the Colorado River. We held tightly to the ropes tied on the raft and screamed with fear and delight as we were buffeted by rapids of various intensity every two or three miles. The majestic mile-high mountainous walls of geologic prehistoric rocks were awesome and humbling. At sunset we camped, ate meals provided by our guide and slept at the side of the river surrounded by the mountains whose eroded peaks at night appeared as ancient temples. My rejection at Yale seemed exquisitely trivial after facing the marvels of nature and visualizing geologic history. My depression was replaced by euphoria at being alive and able to experience the grandeur of the earth.

After a week the group members were lifted from the canyon two campers at a time by a small helicopter; and then bussed to Caesar's Palace in Las Vegas, Nevada. The stark contrast between our pristine life at the bottom of the Grand Canyon and the decadent environment of Caesar's Palace was a peak experience for me. The group felt "bonded" after the trip and we dubbed ourselves "The River Rats." For several years afterwards we vacationed together, usually on rivers with white-water rapids. A month after returning from the invigorating Grand Canyon experience, I received a phone call from Edward Fleming, M.D., a former resident of mine, now President of Psychiatric Institutes of America (P.I.A.) in Washington, D.C., inviting me to join his group in purchasing Elmcrest Manor, a private mental hospital in central Connecticut with the option of my becoming director of the hospital. The offer excited me, and the thought of having unhampered executive power to direct an innovative psychiatric hospital was very tempting. Ella gave her approval and with much trepidation, I accepted Fleming's offer. It required matching PIA's initial financial investment in the venture. I recruited four colleagues and the five of us completed the purchase, and as Marlborough Company, Inc., we assumed a 50 percent joint ownership of Elmcrest Hospital with P.I.A. in September of 1971.

Elmcrest was a fifty-two bed hospital on three acres of landscaped yards, three beautiful stately buildings, an established reputation as a traditional open psychiatric facility catering to adults with a spectrum of mental disorders including depression, anxiety, nonviolent psychoses and alcohol and substance abuse. Nurses wore traditional white uniforms. Electroshock therapy was used frequently and psychiatric medications were heavily prescribed.

I eagerly began direction of the hospital, determined to put into action my version of a therapeutic community as described by Maxwell Jones, M.D. in England (Jones, 1953) and as previously tried by me at the Veterans Hospital in West Haven, Connecticut. A meeting for all the employees of Elmcrest hospital, clinical and non-clinical, was held where I informed all that, in addition to their assigned duties and responsibilities, they were to relate to all the patients as staff co-therapists and also attend my weekly community meetings held with all the patients.

As part of the sale agreement I promised to continue the employment of all existing staff, including the previous medical director and nursing director, both of whom had been there for years. I met with each privately and Dr. Gerard Ryan, an elderly psychiatrist, expressed his skepticism but gave his assurance that he would assist me as best he could as chief of the medical staff. The nursing director, Ms. Bishop, R.N., opened her meeting with me by saying bitterly, "Well, Dr. Fierman, I suppose you want all the nurses here to take off their uniforms!" Distracted by a mental image of a hospital full of nude nurses, I stammered, "No, Miss Bishop, but this is a mental hospital and I don't want them to think they have to wear traditional nursing uniforms if they would rather wear their own personal choice of work clothes."

A few weeks later I discovered that Dr. Ryan was advising his patients in the hospital that they would be better served if they transferred to another hospital. I asked for and received his resignation and Chief Nurse Bishop resigned at the same time. I learned later that they had gone into private practice together.

Despite my previous experience as Chief of Psychiatry at the Veterans Hospital I still felt untrained and inadequate to be CEO of an entire hospital with a staff of over 100 employees. To raise my sense of competence as an administrator, I arranged for consultations with Yale Professor Herbert Shepard. He taught me much about administrative management theory and practice. He also advised that I schedule fifteen-minute interviews with every single employee to inquire into their personal life ambitions, why they were working at Elmcrest and what they would do differently for Elmcrest if they were the CEO. The staff responded with friendly advice and seemed to enjoy their easy access to their director's office.

In addition, I hired my friend, Rachel Robinson, RN, to be Assistant Director of the hospital and Supervisor of the Nursing Service. She is the famous wife of Jackie Robinson, the famous baseball player, and had previously been Director of Nursing at the Yale Connecticut Mental Health Center.

I studied and passed the oral examination needed to be certified in Administrative Psychiatry by the American Psychiatric Association and also arranged for annual weekend workshops for my administrative staff with Pierre Turquet, M.D. Dr. Turquet and his colleague, Mr. A. K. Rice, represented the Tavistock Institute of Human Relations in London, famous for their workshops in England and the USA on group relations and the vicissitudes of power and authority. Because of their reputation in training managers, executives and group therapists, the workshops were attended by administrators of major industries as well as by clinicians concerned with group dynamics.

Ella and I had attended several such workshops in England and the U.S.A., and found them helpful in our administrative tasks and roles. The workshops were strategically designed to place the participants into a microcosm of the world-at-large, where people living and working together organize to perform tasks, elect leaders and establish rules of conduct. Turquet, Rice and their trained assistants served as consultants to the group process, but during group meetings they would only comment on group behavior and would not address nor interact directly with any of the participants as individuals.

At the opening session of the workshop, they would present a brief, terse mandate to the entire large group of approximately fifty participants, saying, "Organize yourselves into small groups and conduct an intergroup exercise. Several rooms are available and a consultant will be in each room to help the group process. The exercise begins now!" They then would leave without answering any questions.

Pandemonium would follow, participants would become confused, agitated and disorganized, scurrying from room to room, searching for the room which they thought would have the alleged best consultant. These rooms were too small to accommodate more than ten or so people. Initially, there was pushing and shoving and no evidence of civility as the group members crowded into the rooms. The consultant in each room would point out to the group the absence of any effort within the group to comply with the stated task of organizing to arrange an intergroup exercise.

This pattern of misbehavior was the basic learning that permeated the entire workshop. The participants learned experientially that in order to perform a group task successfully, they had to rise above the chaos, organize themselves peaceably into small groups, elect leaders and become goal-directed collaborative teams. If the assigned task was ambiguous or poorly defined, as was the case in the workshop, there was a latent negative and destructive force in human groups that would attempt to obstruct the task (the group "mind").

This learning was valuable and applicable to the participants' administrative and management functions in their work lives back home. However, the workshops were stressful because it promoted competition between members to achieve some order and organization in dealing with the obscure task assigned to them.

In every workshop Ella and I attended, there was at least one member who would develop a transient psychotic breakdown. Fortunately, there were many psychiatrists and psychologists among the membership available to treat the brief crises that occurred. Still, a few of the "casualties" would have to leave the workshop to return to their homes and local therapists.

As my own managerial skills improved, I was able to introduce several innovative practices at Elmcrest. I changed the name from Elmcrest Manor to Elmcrest Psychiatric Institute to reflect our teaching and training programs. Then, I asked the clinical staff to agree that the appropriate goal of treatment for all hospitalized patients was not to effect a total cure, but rather to improve the patients' clinical state to the degree that they could be discharged as soon as possible to continue their treatment as outpatients. My rationale was to avoid reinforcing patients' dependency that could result in "hospitalitis" or unnecessarily prolonged hospitalization, especially for those patients prone to dependent behavior.

I wanted Elmcrest to be known as a hospital that emphasized family and group psychotherapy, not just psychopharmacotherapy. Psychiatric medication was used judiciously as an adjunct to psychotherapy, not as the major part of the treatment plan. Nor did I emphasize intense diadic inpatient individual psychotherapy since my concern was that the intense relationship between patient and staff therapist that can occur in individual therapy can prolong hospitalization, and also complicate their referral back to the community psychiatrist or therapist who had referred the patient to us.

Elmcrest was an investor-owned hospital rather than non-profit and depended on the confidence of referring therapists that their patients would be returned to them when discharged. To encourage post-discharge continuity of their therapy, I required that prior to discharge all patients should have one or two appointments with their designated out-patient community psychotherapist. Upon admission, all medications patients were taking were suspended pending review and establishment of their necessity. Some referring psychiatrists complained about this practice until they were assured that their medications would be renewed if found clinically indicated.

Survival of an investor-owned hospital depended on its expenses being less than its income. A large staff of high-salaried psychiatrists was not fiscally sound, so I hired my friend and colleague, Leo Berman, M.D., to organize a psychotherapy training program in which only a few psychiatrists would be needed to train and supervise psychiatric nurses functioning as individual, group and family psychotherapists. Our nurse-therapist program was very popular with nurses and vacancies were easily filled from the many nurses applying for positions at Elmcrest.

Another innovation was to change and redefine the responsibilities of the clinical staff in a way I termed the "Therapist-Administrator Split." This provided each staff clinician with two separate functions: one as administrative therapist for his assigned patient group, and the other as group psychotherapist for a colleague's group. The administrative therapist would be responsible for all management decisions for patients in his assigned group; for example, physical and medical management, medications, passes, privileges, disciplinary issues, scheduling, family relations, discharge planning and the charting of patients' records and files. However, he would not function as the psychotherapist for his own group. Instead, he would function as psychotherapist for a colleague's group of patients and have no responsibility for that group's administrative needs. He could offer confidentiality of the psychotherapy of that group, and would not have to report or document details of the group therapy proceedings. His psychotherapy of his colleague's group would be separate and unrelated to any administrative issues or decisions made by his colleague who would be the administrative therapist for that group and the psychotherapist for his colleague's group.

The rationale and result of this arrangement was that all the patients in the hospital were assigned to a small group of six or seven patients with two staff therapists, one for administrative issues and one for pure group psychotherapy. This permitted the patients to have the nondirective, nonauthoritarian, non-pedagogic, egalitarian relationship with their group psychotherapist necessary for their therapy to be liberating and transformational. Unfortunately, while this nondirective therapy was effective in freeing patients from their need and desire to be hospitalized, in most cases it was not continued by their outpatient therapists after discharge since most therapists in practice provide directive, dependency-reinforcing therapies.

In the course of my tenure as hospital director, in 1974 I persuaded the owners of the hospital to borrow sufficient funds to build separate buildings for adolescent patients, a gym and a Creative Arts Therapy building where patient groups could participate in art, dance and physical therapy programs. The hospital bed capacity gradually increased to 105 beds, and the total staff increased to 350 employees.

A glass greenhouse was used for Horticulture Therapy, provided by Mrs. Nina Pierce, my sister-in-law, whom I had recruited because of her life-long devotion to gardening and her open communicative manner which made her a natural therapist, especially for adolescents. She made the horticulture program more than simply a gratifying pastime, but rather a psychotherapeutic opportunity for patients to relate their work with plants to their personal concerns with creativity, birth, nurturance, growth and death. Her program was very popular with patients of all ages, and over the years it was noteworthy that the glass greenhouse was the only structure on hospital grounds that was spared any breakage or vandalism by patients.

Concern about the evils of tobacco smoking increased throughout the country in the 1970s, and nicotine dependence and addiction were finally added to the official Diagnostic and Statistical Manual of Mental Disorders. Designated smoking areas were established in hospitals but not yet banned when I became Director of Elmcrest. Noticing that many adolescents admitted to Elmcrest were non-smokers but became smokers by the time they were discharged, I felt that hospital staff should serve as role models for adolescent patients, and that seeing hospital nurses and other hospital staff smoking was "enabling" the adolescents to become addicts themselves. I then ruled that hospital staff could no longer smoke in the hospital or on the hospital grounds. Elmcrest thus became the first hospital in Connecticut to ban smoking for staff and visitors.

I was surprised one morning a few days later to receive a phone call from CBS Radio News in New York. The reporter asked if I would consent to being interviewed right then and there on live radio about my smoking ban; apparently news of the ban had rapidly reached New York City. I agreed and we discussed my reasons for the ban. "What happens," he asked, "if you catch one of your employees smoking?" "Where there's smoke," I replied, "there's someone being fired!"

"May I speak to one of your staff about the ban?" he asked.

"Sure," I said, " I'll switch you over to my secretary. "Barbara!" I called out to my secretary in the next room, "Pick up the phone and talk to CBS Radio." I could listen on my phone to Barbara's phone conversation with the reporter. "What do you think of the smoking ban?" he asked. "I think it's ridiculous!" she answered, "If people want to smoke, I think they should have the right to do so!" I was more amused than annoyed, but my staff complied and the ban stood. I arranged for the hospital to pay fifty dollars to any employee who completed the smoke-ending program we provided, but only three employees did so.

All patients who were dependent or addicted to nicotine were required to submit their cigarettes along with their personal supply of medications to the nursing staff upon admission; they were then invited to participate in the smoke-ending programs offered by the hospital. Most patients were voluntary admissions who, while willing to submit to treatment to relieve themselves of psychological and emotional disorders, were not willing to give up cigarettes or enter a smoke-ending treatment program. Rather than attempt a coercive smoke-ending therapy, we agreed that their nurse would dispense their usual daily number of cigarettes along with their prescribed medications. They could then smoke in a designated smoking area in the hospital.

However, the most distinctive and unique program at Elmcrest was the weekly one-hour community meeting for all patients and all staff.[1] Many psychiatric hospitals include a large weekly community group meeting attended by most patients and some of the clinical, nursing, administrative and management staffs, conducted by a clinician and dealing with clinical and administrative problems in the hospital. Elmcrest's community meeting was different and structured as a large group psychotherapy session, not a business meeting. All patients were required to attend, regardless of their competence, diagnosis, willingness or potential for violence. Patients who were noncompliant or regarded as potentially violent were placed in so-called "body bags" and carried by nursing staff into the gym area used for the weekly meetings. All staff and daytime employees of the hospital were required to attend, including maintenance, housekeepers, maids, clinicians, nursing, secretaries and administrative personnel, totaling about 300 people. Hospital personnel had been briefed that their role was to be cotherapists to the patients, to listen and, if they chose, to respond by standing and sharing their reactions and observations with the entire group about the events in the

---

[1] See Appendix 2, p. 127. *"The Community Meeting In a Psychiatric Hospital: The Experimental Use Of a Large Group as Group Psychotherapy.*

meeting or the behavior of the people in the group. No interpretations. No lecturing.

My designate or I would conduct the meeting, initially by stating its purpose to be group psychotherapy with all present encouraged to freely express and share their feelings, thoughts or concerns. No violence permitted. Then I would address all the patients who were in body bags and offer to release them from the constraints of the bags if they would pledge nonviolence and not to disrupt the meeting. Those who consented were released, and if they reneged, staff would immediately replace them in the bag. Those not consenting remained in their bag throughout the meeting. The meeting then was opened and members were invited to share with me or with the group whatever they wished to share.

To qualify as a bona fide psychotherapy, the large community meeting would have to manifest clinical changes in the patient participants. Although no attempt to gather data on behavioral change was ever made, staff and I did observe that patients participating in the weekly meetings over periods of weeks and months did seem to manifest growing trust, openness, excitement, risk taking, counter-phobic behavior and positive feedback, all consistent with the results of an effective group psychotherapy. Impressionistic anecdotal reports and occasional questionnaire surveys also suggested that the community meetings did qualify as a large group psychotherapy.

Of course, the patients used the community meeting not only to promote self-expression and improve their relationships with others, but also to raise complaints about their hospital experience. One such patient, Ms. Joan Smith, a middle-aged, single, depressed librarian, stood up to state: "I want a refund of that part of my hospital charges that covers family therapy,[2] because I'm from California and I have no family in Connecticut. They're all in Los Angeles and I shouldn't have to pay for a therapy I'm not getting."

"Well, Ms. Smith," I responded, "Rather than give you a refund, we will give you a family!" I then asked her to describe her California family. She listed her mother, two sisters and a brother. I then appealed to the hospital staff for volunteers to be a surrogate family for Ms. Smith and to participate with her in the hospital family therapy program. Many employees volunteered from whom Ms. Smith selected four who resembled her family members.

After the meeting she was able to participate along with her ersatz family in the Elmcrest weekly family psychotherapy program. She had briefed the volunteers as to the characteristics of her own family members and her relationship to them, and after a few weeks, reported that her interactions with the volunteers became uncannily similar to the interactions she had actually experienced with her own family. She reported the ability to work through many of the problems and conflicts she had experienced with her own family in California. This merging of family therapy and psychodrama therapy became standard for patients whose families were not available or no longer alive.

The hospital flourished. Our reputation as an innovative treatment and training facility grew. We offered internships for psychologists, training in psychotherapy for nurses, and clerkships for medical students. Hospital directors from around the country would visit and marvel at our dramatic community meetings. The hospital was

---

[2] See Appendix 3, p. 141. *"Family Therapy in Psychiatric Hospital Treatment"*

approved by the Connecticut State Medical Society to provide continuing medical education (CME) for clinicians in the state.

In 1981, after ten years as Medical Director of Elmcrest, I was attracted by an invitation from the Charter Medical Corporation to develop a new mental hospital in Covina, California. After much deliberation I resigned and accepted the offer. My friend and partner, Lane Ameen, M.D., left his full-time position on the Yale faculty to replace me at Elmcrest. He and his clinical director, Anthony Ferrante, M.D. assumed direction of the hospital, expanded the adolescent treatment program and opened a ten-bed unit for pre-teen children. They also opened satellite outpatient clinics in four different cities in the state.

After two years in California I returned to Connecticut to assist Dr. Ameen at Elmcrest and also to resume the position of Medical Director of Psychotherapy Associates, our private practice group in New Haven. In 1997 we received a lucrative offer from St. Francis Hospital of Hartford, Connecticut to purchase the Elmcrest Psychiatric Institute. St. Francis was a well known, reputable general hospital that did not have an inpatient psychiatric service and was eager to buy one rather than develop one on their own. Their management team assumed correctly that Dr. Ameen and I might be tempted to sell the hospital since we both were in our 70s and were old enough to be thinking of retiring. Negotiations proceeded in an orderly fashion and on January 14, 1998, St. Francis Hospital assumed ownership of Elmcrest and changed its name to St. Francis Behavioral Care.

I was proud of Elmcrest's reputation and felt confident that St. Francis Hospital would continue the innovative, humanistic, psychotherapeutic practices that had been established in Elmcrest over the years. It was not to be. Within four years the hospital's reputation for excellent psychiatric care had plummeted. Poor nursing care resulted in two deaths. Dr. Anthony Ferrante, a distinguished child psychiatrist and the hospital's medical director was replaced by a non-psychiatrist physician. The director of nursing, a reputable psychiatric nurse, was replaced by a non-psychiatric general nurse. Children in the hospital who were wards of the state were taken out of the hospital by the state because of the poor quality of care. Staff morale was very low. Referrals from community physicians dropped off; and, finally, on January 1, 2003, the hospital closed down.

At the end of 2003, after fifty-two years of psychiatric private practice, I retired. Looking back over my life, I marvel at the wonder of it all: to be the fifth child of poor immigrant refugees from Russia and Rumania and to be blessed with good health, mind, parents, family, education, career, patients, friends, marriage, wife, children and grandchildren. And it ain't over yet!

EPILOGUE

EPILOGUE

My life on this planet has spanned the years since 1922 and through cataclysmic world events: the Great Depression, World War II, the Holocaust, the nuclear bombing of Hiroshima and Nagasaki, Truman's war in Korea, Nixon's war in Vietnam, Bush Sr.'s war in Kuwait, 9/11 and Bush Jr.'s invasion of Iraq. I've also lived through the momentous medical discoveries of powerful antibiotics and vaccines, open heart surgery, cloning, and organ transplants; plus amazing scientific innovations of television, space travel, computers, the internet and cell phones.

Unfortunately, the human community has not kept pace with the progress made by scientists. Primitive thinking, murderous religious rivalries, and rampant destruction of the world's environment all threaten the future survival of the planet itself. Yet, like a busy ant hill, humans the world over scurry about concerned with their petty problems, oblivious to the crises all about them urgently needing resolution.

Now, in my eighth decade of life, I ask myself, "Okay, Doctor Know-It-All, have you learned anything at all in your life that would be of help for you or others to cope with the exigencies of life that you decry?" My answer, in a word, is, "Love. Love life. Love yourself. Love nature. Love your friends and love your enemies. Love your family. Love creation, of which you are a part, and if you are a physician, love your patients."

The love I speak of is a nurturing, caring, forgiving, empathic and unconditional love. Love that listens to the suffering of others, rejects hate and overcomes fear. Love that becomes the motivating force in life. Love that makes life meaningful.

Appendix 1

On Becoming a Nondirective Psychotherapist[1]

[1] Copyright © 2004 by Douglas William Bower and iUniverse, Inc. Reprinted from *Person-Centered/Client-Centered.*, ed. Doug Bower, 2004, pp. 23-29. Used with permission.

Appendix 1

On Becoming a Nondirective Psychotherapist

Most "schools" of psychotherapy and psychoanalysis rely on directive, interpretive and pedagogic activity as the principal effort of the therapist. These directive and "insight"-oriented therapies have as their common denominator a structured authoritarian relationship between patient or client and therapist. It is tacitly agreed that, in a sense, the patient suffers directly or indirectly from a lack of knowledge about himself, or, to be more precise, about that part of himself which is suppressed, repressed, preconscious or unconscious. Furthermore, that the therapist is more familiar with that part of the patient than the patient is himself; and that, finally, if the therapist can successfully impart his esoteric knowledge of the patient to the patient and perhaps assist him or her by imparting additional relevant knowledge, the patient will use the new-found information to cope with and integrate these heretofore hidden aspects of himself so as to become healthier and happier. In addition to promoting "insight," the therapist can also help the patient by offering directly or indirectly strategic and appropriate direction, guidance, advice and suggestions.

However, some psychotherapists, trained and working within such a structured, strategic, insight or directive framework of psychotherapy, become dissatisfied and disillusioned with these premises. After exhausting the many rationalizations available to account for treatment failures, the conscientious psychotherapist arrives at a turning point in which these basic issues are themselves at stake. Many prominent therapists have gradually shifted and promoted therapies that deviate partially or completely from the Freudian analytic, insight-oriented or directive approach. As an alternative they frequently focus on the here-and-now relationship between therapist and patient rather than on the history and pathogenesis of the patient's mental disorder, and in some cases have abandoned directive activity entirely in performing psychotherapy.

Hellmuth Kaiser, Peter Lomas and Carl Rogers were three such therapists. They all began their careers as psychotherapists using structured, technique-oriented, directive approaches in therapy, but became disenchanted with directive psychotherapy and developed similar models of nondirective psychotherapy that have influenced the practice of psychotherapy throughout the world. As Peter Lomas put it succinctly, they all underwent "departure from Freud" (Lomas, 1981, p. 3).

Hellmuth Kaiser graduated from the Berlin Psychoanalytic Institute in 1929 and was trained to be an orthodox Freudian psychoanalyst. However, he was much influenced by Wilhelm Reich, one of his teachers. Reich taught that psychoanalytic therapy was frequently ineffective because the patient's resistance to change was ingrained in his or her character and personality. He advocated that formal analysis should first be preceded by so-called "character analysis," in which the analyst would confront the patient face-to-face with observations of the patient's overt and covert attitudinal resistances (Reich, 1949).

Kaiser, however, found that therapy became even more effective if, instead of reverting back to orthodox analysis as Reich had taught, he would continue throughout the therapy to confront the patient face-to-face with his overt attitudinal and incongruous communicative behavior. After years of experience, Kaiser gradually became convinced that confrontations seemed to reinforce patients' dependent behavior. He then decided to abandon confrontations, and instead, to simply offer to his patients a here-and-now, non-confrontational, nonjudgmental, nondirective, interactive, communicative-intimacy relationship. He described his gradual evolution to a completely nondirective therapy in his monograph: *The Universal Symptom of the Psychoneuroses: a Search for the Conditions of Effective Psychotherapy* (Kaiser, 1965a).

The Kaiserian therapist disavows as therapeutic activity any explicit pedagogy, interpretation, confrontation or strategic maneuvers. The patient is regarded as being literally free to do in the therapy session whatever he or she pleases. The only limitations are those determined by the therapist's personal needs and interests, such as time, financial arrangements or self-protection. Beyond the therapist's personal limitations, the situation and the relationship are left essentially free and unstructured, and the therapist's activity becomes simply sharing with the patient those of his reactions to the patient's behavior that he deems appropriate.

Kaiser regarded dependency as the core psychopathology of psychoneuroses and he designed his therapy to be nondirective to avoid reinforcing the basic dependency of the patient. "Cure" of the patient was to be achieved by the therapist offering the patient a relationship which I have come to call "communicative-intimacy" (Fierman, 1997). The basic assumption of Kaiserian therapy is that consistent nondirective "genuine" behavior and communication on the part of the therapist is all that is "necessary and sufficient" to effect a cure. This concept is analogous to Carl Rogers' concept of "congruence" as an essential condition for psychotherapists. In this therapy the only "rules" are that the patient be physically present with an intact central nervous system, and that the therapist not withdraw psychologically from his or her patient. The Kaiserian model of therapy seems to meet all the criteria for being identical with Carl Rogers' client-centered therapy.

Similar to both Kaiser and Rogers, Peter Lomas, a prominent psychoanalyst in Cambridge, England, also abandoned orthodox psychoanalysis and advocated instead a "personal psychotherapy." In his book, *The Case for a Personal Psychotherapy* (Lomas, 1981), his rhetoric is analogous to the principles of Rogers' client-centered therapy and Kaiser's communicative-intimacy therapy.

In his book Lomas described what he thought a therapist should not do: "The therapist should not, in a polite or conventional way, smooth over difficulties or (worse) humour the patient or adopt a patronizing bedside manner; nor should he be committed to an opposite dogma—a relentless pursuit of the truth at all costs on all occasions, with an accompanying need to open up old wounds in the interests of theoretical rigor; his primary aim should not be to understand the patient , nor to learn from him, nor to enlarge the frontiers of science through his studies of him, nor to assuage his own loneliness or to seek a substitute for child, spouse, parent or lover. He should not use the patient to treat, vicariously, his own neurosis or as a captive audience for his own particular brand of theory.... The perspective I am here proposing for psychotherapy is ... embarrassingly unspecific ... it refers to a situation in which one person is aiming to help another to grow by offering him a relationship that has much in common with those in ordinary living but takes place in an unusual context" (Lomas, 1981, p. 43-44). Lomas also urged spontaneity and genuineness as crucial qualities for psychotherapists' responses to their patients: "... I have used the term 'spontaneity' to indicate a quality of response that comes—insofar as this is possible—from the core of one's being rather than behavior that has been rehearsed according to a plan, strategy, or theory. It seems likely that, being unrestrained, the spontaneous mode of being would be less of an effort. The difference is akin to that between a formal dinner party in which one feels the need to behave in an acceptable way and meeting an old friend with whom one can leave one's pretenses behind. Such a meeting is not a scientific search for truth but, in some ways, there is more likely to be truth around" (Lomas, 1999, p. 91).

In his book, *The Limitations of Interpretation / What's Wrong With Psychoanalysis*, (Lomas, 1987, p. 4), Lomas disavowed analytic interpretation: "Explanation and interpretation are means by which we may attempt to control and diminish the full force of being." In addition he advocated "intimacy" rather than "insight" as a goal of therapy: "... the most apparent impairment (in patients) is an inability to make sufficiently close and realistic relationships with others. It is primarily for this reason that people consult psychotherapists ... a major task of the therapist is to help his patients towards a greater capacity for intimacy" (Ibid, p. 69).

Finally we come to the great Carl Rogers, the third of the trio of therapists under discussion, all of whom independently arrived at similar innovative, nondirective, humanistic, nonauthoritarian therapies. Carl Rogers was raised in a fundamentalist evangelical farm family, the fourth of six children. In his autobiography, *On Becoming a Person*, he tersely characterizes his early years: "... a very strict and uncompromising religious and ethical atmosphere ... parents were very controlling of our behavior" (Rogers, 1961). He considered theology as a career but then trained as a Freudian psychoanalytically-oriented child psychologist at Columbia University. In 1928 he joined the staff of the Rochester Child Study Department and was influenced by the teachings of Otto Rank to abandon orthodox psychoanalysis. He progressively moved away from any approach in therapy that was coercive, and developed and published his initial concepts of "client centered therapy" in his book *Counseling and Psychotherapy* (Rogers, 1942). He was then much influenced by the concept of the "actualizing tendency" promoted by Maslow and others (Maslow, 1956), and nondirectiveness became the *sine qua non* of Rogerian psychotherapy. He replaced the directiveness of Freud, Otto Rank and other insight-oriented psychoanalytic psychotherapists with what he called "nondirective acceptance." However, he actually was not completely nondirective at that time. Instead, he advocated that the therapist refrain from interactive activity and instead strive to encourage continued catharsis in order to promote the patient's self actualization.

In his book *Client Centered Therapy* (1951) he stated: "The therapist endeavors to keep himself out as a separate person...the counselor being depersonalized for the purposes of therapy into being the client's other self." But over the years Rogers gradually abandoned self-restraint and finally advocated his three "core conditions" for effective therapy: 1) The therapist's unconditional positive regard for the client, 2) The therapist's empathic understanding of the client, and 3) The therapist's congruence. In the 60s he finally advocated as therapy offering the patient a full, open, spontaneous, sharing, empathic and congruent relationship. Rogers wrote: "I had come to recognize quite fully that the therapist must be present as a person in the relationship if therapy is to take place" (Evans, 1975, p. 25). Later he added: "I find that when I am closest to my inner intuitive self...whatever I do seems to be full of healing...simply my *presence* is releasing and helpful to the other" (Rogers, 1980, p. 129).

CONCLUSION

This paper has discussed three prominent therapists who underwent a shift from directive to nondirective therapy; Hellmuth Kaiser, Peter Lomas and Carl Rogers. However, a review of their careers does not reveal exactly just how, why or when that shift occurred. Why, in contrast to most of their professional colleagues and contemporaries, did they become dissatisfied with their previous directive orientation, and why did they end up with such similar humanistic, egalitarian and nondirective therapies? To answer that question we can only speculate as to how their life experiences influenced them to change.

Hellmuth Kaiser was born into and grew up in a well-to-do upper-middle-class intellectual professional German family. He served in the German army during WWI, and on his return he trained and became a Freudian psychoanalyst. But the anti-Semitic ravages of Hitler's brutal Nazism drove him out of Germany, a stateless, penniless refugee who made his way to Israel and then to the USA, sponsored by Karl Menninger. Perhaps his anger toward his ungrateful, bigoted and authoritarian fatherland helped to fuel his rebellion from authoritarian Freudian psychoanalysis.

Peter Lomas received his M.D. at Manchester University in England, and was a general practitioner before entering the London Institute of Psychoanalysis. He gradually became disillusioned with orthodox analysis after studying the works of Buber and other existential philosophers and therapists, and cites these authors and teachers as persuading him to "depart from Freud."

Carl Rogers experienced in his childhood excessive parental control and religious constrictions, and this may well have contributed to his later aversion to coercion and his discarding all strategic, goal-directed activity from his therapies. Another possible and plausible answer to the riddle of accounting for this shift of these and other therapists to a nondirective, humanistic therapy came from my wife, Ella Yensen Fierman, Ph.D., a clinical psychologist and psychotherapist: "I think they were influenced by their patients," she speculated, "particularly those patients who were able to express their desire to have an egalitarian, open, genuine, nondirective, communicative-intimacy relationship with their therapists. Therapy is a two-way street. Patients can and do influence their therapists and sometimes even free them from their authoritarian constraints" (Fierman, E., 2003).

Her insightful statement reminded me of Hellmuth Kaiser's short play *"Emergency"* (Kaiser, 1962). Kaiser wrote this playlet to illustrate his contention that the active ingredient of effective psychotherapy was the communicative relationship between therapist and patient and not a function of their relative status or expertise. In the play an imposter patient treats a therapist psychotherapeutically as part of a strategy secretly arranged by the therapist's wife. But I believe the same scenario could just as well have occurred even if the patient were an actual patient who decided to treat his therapist without being hired to do so by a third party.

Irvin Yalom (2002) also has written about occasions when patients have treated their therapists psychotherapeutically. Similarly, Peter Lomas wrote: "The dependence of patients is often the most hazardous ordeal which a psychotherapist has to face" (1981, p. 145). He cites instances when he felt pressured by his patients to become more open, personal and communicative.

Martin Buber maintained that in an I-Thou relationship there is "healing in the meeting" that promotes improved mental health in both patient and therapist and makes the experience of psychotherapy gratifying and nurturing (Buber, 1970).

Appendix 2

The Community Meeting in a Psychiatric Hospital: The Experimental Use of a Large Group as Group Psychotherapy[1]

Appendix 2

The Community Meeting in a Psychiatric Hospital: The Experimental Use of a Large Group as Group Psychotherapy

The inclusion in psychiatric hospital practice of a therapeutic community program modeled after the work of Caudill (1958), Edelson (1970), Fairweather (1969), Jones (1953), Rioch (1953), and others has become commonplace. Therapeutic community programs usually include regularly scheduled community meetings attended by all or most patients in the hospital-at-large, or from designated units, and by all or part of the clinical, nursing, administrative and management staffs of the hospital or unit. These institutional events are large group meetings subject to large group dynamics. Conventionally, they are conducted as task-oriented work groups concerned with identification, clarification and resolution of clinical and administrative problems existent in the hospital.

The author had participated in several Tavistock model group relations training conferences involving large study group exercises. He had observed that in these experiential conferences the large group behavior engendered by the non-directive task "to study large group behavior as it occurs" consistently produced among its participants spontaneous communicative interaction, intense emotional impact, "unfreezing" of stereotyped role behavior and other dramatic behavioral changes. He postulated that community meetings in a psychiatric hospital conducted nondirectively along similar bases as large study group exercises over sufficient period of time would constitute an effective group psychotherapy experience.

As newly appointed (1971) medical director of a private psychiatric hospital (Elmcrest Psychiatric Institute, Portland, Connecticut) with 52 beds in 1971, expanded to 105 beds in 1974, he introduced an intensive therapeutic community program into the hospital. The program included a weekly one-hour community meeting for all patients and staff, which he designated as a large group psychotherapy meeting rather than as a work or business meeting. The primary task of this community meeting continues to be identified to patients and staff as group psychotherapy, but the meetings are conducted, more or less, as a large study group exercise might be, with staff serving collectively as therapists-consultants to the large study group. Staff interventions are offered in the spirit of sharing reactions and observations rather than as interpretations or pedagogy. The content of staff remarks frequently takes the form of group process interpretations as well as revelations of personal affective or cognitive reactions, observations and associations. Over the years since 1971 the author's hypothesis has been confirmed experientially; namely, that phenomena characteristic of large study group exercises in group relations training conferences do consistently occur in the large group psychotherapy/community meetings of the hospital. In addition, while chaotic, disruptive, aggressive or hostile behaviors frequently occur, persistent counter-themes of humanistic concern, rescue and support operations, and caring and nurturing behavior characteristic of effective group psychotherapy also frequently occur. Patients participating in the weekly community meeting over periods of weeks and months seem to experience growing trust and openness, excitement and risk taking, counterphobic behavior and positive feedback, all consistent with group psychotherapy phenomena. The experiences in the community meeting frequently are integrated afterwards by the patients with other experiences received in their small group and family therapies during the rest of the hospital treatment program. Finally, impressionistic reports and a questionnaire survey also support the contention that the community meeting constitutes an effective large group psychotherapy.

The proposition that a large group meeting conducted along these lines would provide an effective psychotherapy is not dealt with extensively in the literature. Freud's original article on group psychology (1921) emphasized the importance of identification with the leader. Freud referred to previous studies by LeBon on the psychology of crowds. LeBon made the point that the behavior of people in large groups simulates that of primitive peoples and children. American clinicians who developed modern concepts of group dynamics and therapy included Burrow (1927), Lewin (1935), Moreno (1958), Schilder (1938), Slavson (1947, 1956), and others. British contributions came from Bion (1959), Ezriel (1950),

Foulkes (1964), and others. Rapoport (1960) wrote on the use of community meetings in psychiatric hospitals for social control. Rice and Turquet began large group study exercises in 1957, and described them in their book *"Learning for Leadership"* (1965). A study by Curry (1967) concluded that psychotherapy could not occur satisfactorily in a large group situation. However, Kreeger (1975), in his book *The Large Group: Dynamics and Therapy* (1974), observed that the large group can be enormously stimulating and provocative of real creative, original thought, and that in all hospitals or institutions that try to function as therapeutic communities, the large group or community meeting is a sine qua non of the culture. He also observed that in large group experiences psychotic mechanisms abound, and people reported that just the experience of being in a large group puts them more clearly in touch with the primitive aspects of their own personality than any other therapy situation. Furthermore, that participating in a large group can add significantly to fuller understanding of oneself and in turn to an increased awareness of personality development and definition of individual psychopathology.

Turquet (1975) described the threat to personal identity experienced by individuals in large group situations. Edelson (1970) firmly espoused the position that psychotherapy was not possible in large groups. However, he did advocate that "sociotherapy" was possible, defining psychotherapy as dealing with problems and tensions between and within individuals, and sociotherapy as dealing with intra- and inter-group tensions. Kreeger (1975) and others have differed with him and charged that his definitions are too rigid, and that the experience and outcome of large group clinical meetings support the contention that a large group psychotherapy is possible and effective.

Carl Rogers (1977) reported on "person-centered" group therapy with a group of over 600 people during a one-week workshop. Most of the week was spent in this unstructured huge encounter group. He did this in the spirit of trial and experiment, and his description of the events parallels our own experience with our weekly community meetings attended by over 120 patients and staff. Rogers identified various phases in his large group therapy: chaotic beginning, gradual development of group cohesiveness, growing humanistic concern between members, and finally, by the time the week was over, a cohesive and established therapy group with very poignant interchanges between participants in that setting.

At Elmcrest patients and staff participated in a questionnaire evaluation of the weekly one-hour community meetings. The study was designed to assess staff and patient reactions to, and judgments of, the community meeting as a form of group psychotherapy, and to identify some of the variables affecting those reactions, such as length of staff employment and patients' length of stay, staff's professional discipline or department and previous Tavistock group relations training. Written opinions and recommendations concerning the Community Meeting were also solicited for the study (Minear, 1979).

The results of the questionnaire evaluation indicate general agreement (65%) among the professional staff that the weekly community meeting does qualify as an effective group psychotherapy. Thirty-five percent of staff rated its effects as either neutral or harmful. Patients were about evenly divided in this judgment. Neither length of employment at Elmcrest nor professional department or discipline proved significant in determining this judgment. There was, however, a significant positive relation-

ship between having had previous Tavistock group relations training and the more favorable ratings. Patient's
length of stay also was found not to be related to patient's
ratings of how the community meeting contributed to
their treatment experience.

Several major themes favorable to the community
meeting appeared in the staff's narrative responses on the
questionnaire. Using such terms as "barometer," "pulse,"
"atmosphere" and "emotional climate," staff members
reported obtaining a useful sense of the attitudinal dispo-
sition of patients in the hospital-at-large through observing interactions between the various sub-groups in the
meetings. A sense of community and family was reported.
The meetings provided opportunities for self-expression
and self-exploration, inter- and intra-unit confrontations,
sharing and receiving helpful feedback. The community
meeting was acknowledged as an opportunity to learn
about one's own reactions to anxiety-producing situations. Others commented on enjoying the frequent humorous and entertaining experiences occurring in the
meetings. The community meeting also was appreciated
as a "gathering of the clan," providing a sense of family,
community and continuity. Staff members reported enjoying the weekly encounter with colleagues, fellow clinicians, new employees and old and new patients of the
hospital.

Prevalent criticisms of the community meeting were
its non-directiveness, lack of structure and organization,
and occasional lack of control with resulting group chaos,
fragmentation, negativism and threats of violence. Some
staff complained of high anxiety resulting from the "intense, disorganized, emotional experience, usually with
lack of closure." Some experienced concern over the fear
of escalating acting-out behavior. Some complained that

the meeting occasionally became "an arena for inter-staff political chicanery, egotistical exhibitionism and attempts to confuse, frighten and mislead patients." Others expressed dissatisfaction with the community meeting as fostering post-meeting chaos, disorder and disruption in patients, and producing feelings of tension and anxiety in staff.

A pervasive positive theme expressed by patients was that the community meeting brought together the entire hospital community and offered a chance to meet and give and receive feedback from one another. Patients commented that the meeting encouraged freedom of expression and discussion of any issue by any member of the community. Patients expressed enjoyment over the fellowship and opportunity to see colleagues and friends from other units, meeting patients newly admitted and being brought up to date on hospital news. Many patients also regarded the meeting as entertaining or humorous diversion from their daily intensive therapy schedule. One patient summed up, "I enjoy hearing about other units, seeing new and familiar faces, hearing about current activities; I feel that I belong after each community meeting."

DISCUSSION

The question of validation of the proposition that the community meeting can be conducted as an effective large group psychotherapy remains unanswered. Methodological problems of evaluating psychotherapy are well known, particularly when the prescription, so-to-speak, is multi-factorial, as is the case with the many components of treatment at Elmcrest. It is possible to assess the overall treatment program in terms of "before and after" clinical assessment of patients. Such studies simply measure treatment outcome in terms of the patient's follow-up clinical state after discharge. But to compartmentalize that result and evaluate separately such components of treatment as chemotherapy, family therapy, community meetings, small group therapy or individual therapy, would be a formidable, if not impossible, task and this has not been addressed in this report. The rationale, then, of ascribing therapeutic value to any particular component of the treatment program rests on the context of that activity, its process and phenomenology plus the patient's immediate responses to that component of therapy. Thus, if a patient is, for example, in art therapy, and during the time spent there becomes symptom-free, stimulated, socialized, communicative, experimental and creative, we then would feel justified to judge that experience as a therapeutic one even though we might not know the duration, outcome or generalizability of the patient's responses. That is to say, we would be willing to view patients' immediate responses to art therapy sessions as presumptive evidence that the experience of art therapy does qualify as a therapy.

This, then, is the rather thin rationale for stating that the large group community meeting does qualify as a group psychotherapy, namely, that the behavioral responses of patients in the context of the meeting appear to be consistent with therapeutic experience. The community meetings seem consistently to produce spontaneous communicative interactions, intense emotionality, unfreezing of stereotyped behavior with new adaptive behavior occurring on the part of participants. Descriptions of the community meetings also suggest a common ground with small group psychotherapy: chaotic beginnings with disjointed, unrelated expressions of affect-laden complaints are gradually replaced by struggles for focus, structure and leadership. The struggle is accompanied by expressions of frustration, anger and disappointment, but, finally, there is gradual emergence of sustained, patterned sharing and supportive relevant responsiveness. This process also has been described by Rogers (1977). The large therapy group seems to move with much difficulty and tension toward building a supportive, nurturing therapeutic community. The meetings frequently end on a single focus, theme or person as the group's agenda. This sequence characterizes many of our community meetings. They start as chaotic, followed by gradual pulling together around a theme or person, with final ending on a high level of synchronized coordination among the various subgroups. A sense of togetherness, competence, strength and excitement prevails in the group's mastery over chaos and negativity.

Staff contributions include role modeling and verbal sharing of inner responses and concerns. Simple descriptive observations of group behavior stated in a non-judgmental way seem to contribute to the organizing process and promote implicit and explicit attitudes of trust among patients and staff. The concern, respect, positive regard, and focus on process rather than content or outcome, characterize staff interventions. The willingness by staff to accept patients as a group of persons with common and shared concerns, needs and aspirations is essential. The staff conveys trust that the group will find its own way, its own strength, its own purpose and leadership without staff imposing condescending leadership or structure upon them.

Large group experiences can be powerful, dramatic and profound for all categories of participants, not only when the participants are competent credentialed professions, as in a Tavistock conference, but even when the group consists of hospitalized, severely disordered mental patients, half of them adolescents. The normalizing, socializing, anti-psychotic, anti-neurotic, anti-dependency effects of the experience qualify the large group community meeting as a potent form of group psychotherapy.

The large group not only can be an effective group psychotherapy, but also is an effective sociotherapy as defined by Edelson (1970). The large group meeting does promote resolution of inter- and intra-group tensions and conflicts. The sub-groups of the hospital are in continuous inter-play. Individuals become spokesmen in the community meeting for their sub-groups, such as their ward or units, their age group, diagnosis or behavior pathology. The differences between large group and small group psychotherapy appear to be insignificant. There seems to be no compelling reasons why the rationale for small group psychotherapy should not also apply to large group psychotherapy.

A frequent criticism of the community meeting being conducted as a large group therapy is that it is too stressful, that it is not easily controllable by the therapists and that there is too much risk of violence. However, one could make the case that all effective psychotherapies require the introduction of some stress in terms of the therapy threatening the patient's behavioral status quo. The therapist and the therapy are pitted against the defenses and neurotic behavior patterns of the patient. Thus, built into psychotherapy is always something like a struggle. The competence of therapists includes being able to titrate that stress and keep it at a constructive level rather than as a destructive, pathogenic or catastrophic experience.

In a general sense the community meeting as therapy offers patients an opportunity for differentiation and autonomization. It may be a fearful experience to stand up and speak in the community meeting, but to do so does increase the patient's sense of autonomy and individuality. Patients can be observed as becoming more and more differentiated and less and less fused with their group as their hospital experience evolves. In the preface to his book, *The Large Group: Dynamics and Therapy* (1974), Lionel Kreeger wrote that the whole field of psychotherapy is rapidly expanding and in the last decade interest has been turning towards the large group. As a result of including large group experience both in therapeutic institutions and training schemes, the potential of this technique begins to emerge. All those who have worked with large groups will acknowledge the fascination and power that they hold and most would agree that they present a new dimension to our understanding of group dynamics. The place of large group therapy was still to be defined (Kreeger, 1975).

Appendix 3

Family Therapy in Psychiatric Hospital Treatment[1]

Appendix 3

Family Therapy in Psychiatric Hospital Treatment

Prior to 1960 treatment of the families of hospitalized psychiatric patients was mainly concerned with allaying guilt and other feelings associated with the mental illness of the identified patient. The psychiatric social worker within a hospital setting would obtain the clinical history from family members and also answer questions by the family regarding hospital routine. Family involvement in intake or subsequent treatment was usually peripheral and rarely routine. Even in child guidance clinics, families were rarely involved in the treatment process, but rather, using a team approach, the psychiatrist saw the child, the social worker dealt separately with the family, and the psychologist would administer psychological tests to the child. This compartmentalization of the family usually excluded the father entirely. When family therapy was used in hospital treatment, it was largely adjunctive, something secondary to the individual psychotherapy, group therapy, or biological or physical therapies being offered.

However, in the '50s, work with schizophrenic patients by a number of clinicians led to new awareness of the importance of the family in terms of pathogenesis, pathology and treatment. Murray Bowen (1957, 1961, 1965) called for involvement of families in the therapeutic process, and, coincidentally, Ackerman and Behrens (1956, 1958), Jackson (1958), Satir (1964), and Whitaker (1967) also wrote on this subject, laying the groundwork for a theory and practice of family therapy. Others, such as Bateson and colleagues (1956), Framo (1975), Haley (1963), Lidz (1968), Minuchin (1975), Watzlawick and colleagues (1957), and Wynne (1965) should be mentioned.

Family therapy practice also was influenced by the "human potential" and encounter group movements of the 1950s and 1960s. These developments led to the evolving of a "here and now," active interventionist approach in family therapy and contributed to the establishment of family therapy as a primary sub-specialty in clinical psychiatry, psychology, and social work. J. L. Moreno's work (1946) in reconstructing family history in psychodrama contributed to the subsequent development of family therapy theory. The application of general systems theory to the field of human behavior by L. Von Bertalanffy (1966) also played a part in the evolution of family therapy.

However, in the course of its evolution as a major component of psychosocial treatment, family therapy theory and practice split into two alternative models, paralleling the conflicting models of individual and group psychotherapy; namely, between directive and non-directive approaches. Orientations that lent themselves to directive and strategic interventions in family therapy derived from the work of Minuchin, Haley, Bowen, Papp and Watzlawick. They espoused strategic, directive, and active interventions for problem solving by family therapists. They also proposed strategic and directive interventions by the therapist to change basic family configurations. The school of family therapy that rejects and opposes strategic, directive interventionist approaches seems to have fewer proponents than the directive strategic mode. Virginia Satir and Carl Whitaker are well known representatives of the non-strategic approach. This group of therapists espouses a more existential, humanistic, non-authoritarian stance, emphasizing and offering spontaneous interpersonal intimacy and communication by the therapist as the preferred approach for effective family therapy. Non-strategic family therapists show relatively less concern than the directive schools for explicit or direct problem solving in treatment, and view problem solving by the family as an outcome of therapy rather than as a focus or goal of therapy itself.

Christian Beels and Andrew Ferber (1969) have classified family therapists on the basis of what they call conductors or reactors. They also subdivide the reactor group into analysts and systems purists. We note that Beels and Ferber categorize Virginia Satir as a conductor.

A FAMILY-ORIENTED PSYCHIATRIC HOSPITAL

As newly appointed (1971) Medical Director of a private psychiatric hospital with fifty-two beds in 1971, expanded to 105 beds in 1974, the author decided to design and implement a family therapy program for all patients admitted to the hospital. The author was not only influenced by the family therapists cited above, but also by the

concepts of nondirective psychotherapy developed by
Hellmuth Kaiser (Fierman, ed., 1965). Kaiser was a training psychoanalyst who, late in his career, shifted from
traditional psychoanalytic techniques to an existential,
communicative, non-directive stance in his therapy.
Murray Bowen was influenced by Kaiser while both were
teaching at the Menninger Foundation, and Bowen's
theories on de-differentiation of family members contain
elements of Kaiser's fusion theories. A Kaiserian approach applied to family therapy defines the task of the
family therapist simply as providing a communicative
experience by the therapist for all the members of the
family. The intent of the therapy is to move all family
members in the direction of becoming "defused," that is,
to facilitate the freeing of each family member from fusion
relationships with one another by accepting themselves
(or more precisely, to stop denying themselves) as differentiated, separate individuals in their family. Using this
communicative approach the family therapist invites all
the members of the family to relate as therapists to one
another, thereby making each family therapy session an
experience in intimate interpersonal encountering.

FAMILY THERAPY AS GROUP THERAPY

Using Kaiser's orientation, the essence of intra-family
pathology is conceptualized as being that family members
relate to one another as though they were fused and inter-
connected, and as though the focus of power and decision
making for each individual family member was somehow
projected into members other than themselves. Family
members do not function as separate and autonomous
beings within their family.

The goal of this family therapy is the same as the goal of group psychotherapy, namely, to promote psychological separateness, autonomy, maturity and independence in its members. This is done both in family and group psychotherapy by freeing family or group members from their patterns of relating to other people in a fused way which distorts the reality of their individuality and separateness. The presence of actual family members in family therapy facilitates the therapeutic process of group therapy. These concepts are similar to Bowen's theory of the undifferentiated family ego mass resulting from pathological triangular relationships leading to family behavior pathology. Thus, group therapy may be conceptualized as surrogate family therapy. Similarly, family therapy may be conceptualized as group therapy with actual family members present. This line of reasoning has led the author to use surrogate family therapy for hospitalized patients who, for one reason or another, have no family members to participate in family therapy. Volunteer staff members, uninvolved in the patient's treatment, serve as surrogate family members in ongoing family therapy.

FAMILY THERAPY FOR DISCHARGE PLANNING

Family therapy in hospital settings is relevant to both of the two principal functions of hospitalization; namely, to provide effective psychosocial therapy as well as competent administrative management of the patient. It is important that the management of the patient be differentiated conceptually and instrumentally from his psychotherapy. Management of the hospitalized patient is, of necessity, goal-directed, symptom-oriented, and con-

cerned with discharge planning and the return and rehabilitation of the patient to his home and community. These
goals of patient management should be differentiated
from the goal of psychotherapy which is to promote
psychological autonomy, independence and freedom
from neurotic response patterns. Psychotherapy is cure-
oriented and extends far beyond the period of hospitalization. The work of patient management and patient psychotherapy are ideally done by separate staff members.
The patient's administrative therapist ideally should not
be the patient's psychotherapist. There are considerable
advantages in conceptualizing the two approaches and
goals differently and separately, and also negative conse-
quences in failing to do so. Power struggles, resistance to
therapy, acting-out, and non-compliance are facilitated
by having the same individuals function as both administrative therapists and psychosocial therapists. Family
therapy, however, is relevant to both administrative and
psychotherapeutic goals. Family therapy can provide not
only a potent and effective psychotherapy, but also can
provide a format for effective patient management and
discharge planning. Issues concerning discharge depend
heavily on the state of affairs within the patient's family.
Discharge planning is best begun at the time of admission,
and the patient's family should be invited to participate.

DISADVANTAGES OF INPATIENT
FAMILY THERAPY

One major disadvantage of family therapy in hospitals
is, of course, that the patient and the family must meet the
heavy financial burden of hospitalization in addition to
the costs of therapy. Another major disadvantage is that
the hospitalized family member can hardly avoid being

identified by others in the family as the "sick" member, thereby facilitating the resistance of other family members to deny their own psychological disorder or need for change or therapy.

Ideal family therapy sees all members of the family as separate, albeit inter-dependent individuals in a family social system that has failed to permit all of its members to experience optimum mental health and reach full human potential. The hospitalized patient has been separated physically from his family, community and job, and although this may be unavoidable because of the severity of the patient's disability, it creates problems in its own right and tends to foster dependency on the institution. Also, the unavoidable turnover of patients, groups and staff therapists in the hospital introduces instability into the family therapy experience.

ADVANTAGES OF INPATIENT FAMILY THERAPY

The advantages of family therapy for inpatients are very significant. The authority of the hospital plus the crisis situation of the patient greatly facilitates involving the family and significant others in the patient's treatment. Hospital therapists can schedule intensive, high frequency psychotherapy with sessions several times a week or even daily. Family therapy within the hospital is done in a controlled environment. In a hospital therapeutic community the patient's patterns of relating to others can be more easily related to his family therapy.

Multiple family therapy is a valuable supplement to individual family therapy and is easily arranged during hospitalization (Haley et al., 1974) The patient and his family meet at least weekly with other patients and their families in a large group therapy. The families relate to one another in ways usually found to be supportive, informative and therapeutic.

RATIONALE FOR FAMILY THERAPY ORIENTED HOSPITAL

The rationale for prescribing family therapy for all hospitalized psychiatric patients is the theory that all psychopathology and behavior pathology is derived either entirely or in part from one's family of origin, and reinforced and exacerbated in the context of one's family of procreation. The issues of growth and development in family life are so central and crucial to the development of psychological health or disorder that the decision to prescribe family therapy as a basic part of treatment for all hospitalized psychiatric patients seems compelling, and has been confirmed clinically.

A hospital treatment program including intensive family therapy for all inpatients is possible for reasonably low cost. Families should be urged at time of the patient's admission to come to the hospital for therapy at least three times a week, including multiple family therapy once a week.

SURROGATE FAMILY THERAPY

To patients for whom all significant family members are absent, deceased, uncooperative or too distant, the hospital offers surrogate family therapy. The patient selects hospital staff and other patients who agree to participate as surrogate family members. The result is a combination of psychodrama and family therapy. This experiment has had favorable results and is now done routinely at the hospital. On one occasion a patient was admitted into the hospital by court order because of delinquency and violent behavior. He reported that he had no family relatives who were willing to have any connections with him, but that he was a member of a Hell's Angels motorcycle gang. The staff invited his Hell's Angels group to come to the hospital to serve as his surrogate family in family therapy. Each day these youths would roar up to the hospital en masse on their motorcycles garbed in their black leather jackets and proceed to function effectively as his family in therapy.

SIMULTANEOUS ADMISSION OF MULTIPLE FAMILY MEMBERS

Another innovation in the use of family therapy in this hospital has been the practice of admitting two or more members of a family simultaneously or during overlapping periods. Over the past eight years approximately forty-five multiple family members were admitted. Of the forty-five, only about five family units were admitted simultaneously, that is, two or more members of the family admitted on the same day. The other instances were when additional family members were admitted days after the initial family member was admitted. This usually was a result of the impact of family therapy itself on the other family members. That is, the initial patient would be admitted to the hospital, and as family therapy evolved it became clear that the identified patient was not the only, or even the most disturbed or disordered or needy person in the family and so a second and, on some occasions, a third member of the family subsequently would be admitted. A modus operandi was established in the hospital to try, whenever possible, to assign the members of the family to different wards or units in the hospital. The individual family members thus would live in different units, but their family therapy arrangements are combined by negotiations between the staffs of the different units. The rationale is to provide the structure for separation for each family member, and to prevent coercion and intimidation between the various family members. Each family member has a base for separate living plus opportunity for as much family interaction and family therapy as seems helpful.

Family members were admitted simultaneously when they were referred for hospitalization as a family unit. In each of these instances they were pairs: husband and wife, two sisters, mother and daughter, and two brothers. In other instances family admissions occurred as fallout from family therapy. The combinations of subsequent admissions included: husband and wife, father and son, father and daughter, mother and son, mother and daughter, and brother and sister.

CASE HISTORY

A thirty-seven-year-old woman was admitted because of expressed suicidal preoccupation. Her husband had left her five years previously and she had become increasingly alcoholic and depressed. Her husband had remarried but maintained intermittent contact with his two daughters, ages twenty and fifteen. Mother was in individual therapy for a year, but her course deteriorated and she was finally hospitalized. The older daughter, now age twenty, dropped out of college. Depressed over her parents' divorce, she had trouble adjusting at college and felt rejected by her peers. During family therapy she confessed suicidal preoccupation and was admitted within a week after her mother. The fifteen-year-old younger daughter became agitated and, during sessions of family therapy, admitted to being heavily involved in drug abuse and was conflicted over peer pressures. She was admitted three weeks after her sister, one month after her mother. Each family member was housed in separate hospital units: the youngest on an adolescent unit, the twenty-year-old on an adult unit, and the mother in another adult unit. They were prescribed daily family therapy sessions together, as well as group therapy separately. They all participated in the hospital-wide therapeutic community programs. The divorced father was persuaded to join the family therapy along with his new wife. There were heavy emotional confrontations, expressions and externalization of much suppressed feelings of resentment towards one another, and towards the parents and their divorce by the children. As family therapy progressed there was gradual reconciliation between family members, and, approximately two months later, the mother left the hospital to continue treatment with her outside therapist. Family therapy continued for the daughters after the mother left the hospital. One week later the oldest daughter left to return to college and continued individual therapy there. One month later the youngest daughter, who had been attending the hospital school, left the hospital and, since then, all have continued with family therapy in their home town.

In some instances involving married couples admitted simultaneously, the couple was assigned initially to separate units. Later on, after therapies have been successful in bringing about change in their relationship, the couple then was moved into the same hospital unit and provided with a private room to share. This practice prevents the couple from being forced to be together prematurely at the outset of their hospital experience.

FAMILY THERAPY FOR PATIENTS WITH ACUTE PSYCHOTIC BEHAVIOR

Another innovative or experimental use of family therapy in the hospital is in the admitting unit when a violent, agitated, disorganized, disoriented, acutely psychotic patient is brought in. Rather than chemical restraints, physical restraints are preferred to immobilize the patient, leaving him available for intensive psychosocial therapy including family therapy. Psychotic behavior is viewed as purposeful communication rather than as irrational behavior. Chemotherapy for behavioral control is used as a last resort, only after psychosocial intervention is tried first, and an intensive marathon family therapy in the Admitting Unit is attempted. In a fair number of trials the patient has been "talked down," and violence decompressed after hours of therapy time by staff and family. Psychotic patients have been returned to a more rational and communicative state of mind within a few days of intensive psychosocial intervention including marathon family therapy sessions.

MOTIVATING FAMILIES FOR INPATIENT FAMILY THERAPY

At time of admission there is usually a great deal of emotional investment by the family to have their relative admitted for treatment. This is a strategic time to motivate families to commit themselves to family therapy. The family is told at that time that they are expected to participate fully in the treatment program. Arrangements for time and frequency of sessions are made. If the family has not accompanied the patient during admission, they are phoned and told their relative has been hospitalized and that their participation in therapy is required. The tension and sense of crisis during the admission process is used as effective leverage for family involvement. Studies have shown that there is little correlation between need for hospitalization and diagnosis, severity of illness or degree of disability. But one consistent factor in hospitalization is the attitude of the family towards the patient in regard to hospitalization itself. The family's desire to extrude this member plus the member's wish to leave the family determines his hospitalization. Conversely, the family's desire to receive him back home plus the patient's wish to leave determines his discharge. Obviously, other factors are involved as well, such as diagnosis and degree of disability. But if the family is willing to accommodate itself to even horrendous and difficult behavior by a family member at home, they can and will do so. A significant part of the admission process involves motivating the family for family therapy. Family therapy is often scheduled for evenings or late afternoons to accommodate working family members.

Non-compliance by family members is remarkably rare, but may occur initially or after a few days or weeks after family therapy has begun. However, much pressure can be brought to bear to prevent this. Strategic pressure is placed upon the patient, who is held responsible for family non-compliance. Frequently it is the patient himself who is overtly or covertly discouraging family members from coming. It is assumed that if the patient really wants the family there, he is able to see that they attend. Frequently, family members will drop out because they find the experience too threatening or traumatic, rather than lack of interest in the patient. The therapist must deal with these issues by anticipating, recognizing and confronting non-compliance and helping the family externalize and verbalize their concerns.

TRAINING STAFF FOR FAMILY THERAPY

Nursing personnel including mental health workers are assigned to a program of training in family therapy. A full year of training is required before one can actually function as a primary family therapist, but, during that year each trainee participates as co-therapist with a senior therapist, and receives didactic, video tape and workshop training. Psychologists, social workers and psychiatrists also provide family therapy and also function as consultants, teachers, supervisors and co-therapists for nursing personnel.

A prime task of senior clinical staff is that of the supervision and training of the family therapists. This has led to some difficulties. The number of trained and skilled family therapists is small, and to locate family therapists who can also teach has been an important consideration in the hospital's hiring practices. A number of difficulties occur in the training program. Nurses and mental health workers had been hesitant about taking on the roles of therapists, but once they overcome their initial fears, they tend to swing to the other pole and behave as if anything and everything they do could be called therapy. This requires continuous supervision and training of such personnel. It also necessitates an on-going training program for the senior clinicians so that they can continue to acquire the skills required to deal with their trainees.

CONCLUSION

The primary task of inpatient family therapy is to provide psychotherapeutic experiences for the hospitalized patient. Patients enter the hospital in crisis. The goal of hospital treatment and management is to effect the earliest possible return to the community and to motivate the patient to continue treatment after discharge to prevent relapse and readmission. Prerequisite for discharge is a firm discharge plan which includes identification and actual contact with a follow-up individual and/or family therapist who sees the patient several times prior to discharge from the hospital. There should be overlapping of inpatient and outpatient therapy experiences. Issues concerning discharge become the initial focus of family therapy. However, as therapy evolves, the focus shifts to core conflicts within the family as well as rehabilitation, vocational and adjustment issues of the patient. Inpatient family therapy provides a crucial and potent contribution to both effective psychiatric hospital treatment and effective discharge planning. These are the two essentials of successful hospital treatment.

Appendix 4

Letter from Japan

Appendix 4

Letter from Japan

This is a literal copy of the narratives in my letter of January 10, 1948 from Japan to my wife, Ella, in Lyndhurst, Ohio, commenting on the forty photographs which accompanied the text of the letter.

After a week at the replacement depot in Zama, I was assigned to military gov't. as Port Quar. officer and was sent to Yokohama for two weeks' training. While there I lived at the Rising Sun Hotel—in front of which you see Lt. McGill of Louisiana— a fellow medic.

I reported each morning to the Yokohama port for instruction, as did Lt. Maniglia of New York.

*When not working, we loafed or went to the football games
held at Lou Gehrig Stadium in Yokohama.*

One Sunday, Lt. Frank Cebul of Cleveland, Ohio (whom I bumped into in the Yokohama PX— he was stationed in Yokohama 155th Station Hospital) and I visited nearby Tokyo. Frank is standing in front of the Imperial Hotel—where the Emperor lives when not in his palace.

I pause in front of the Emperor's palace—the palace wall is to my right—and in the distance is the Dai Ichi building—the headquarters for Doug. MacArthur and his staff.

Here I am closer to the same building.

Japanese are leaving a theater—while we walk about the streets of Tokyo.

Getting tired of walking, I call a taxi.

*Finally orders come
to report to Kyoto
for final assign-
ment. While waiting
for further orders, I
visit some Buddhist
temples in Kyoto ...*

and watch the Japanese watching a foot-race of small children in the park.

By drawing names from a hat, I become assigned to Fukuoka MGT, and after arriving get my first view of the valley overlooking which is Kajima House, my new home—

and not bad.

A dog guards the entrance against trespassers.

I meet my maids: Annie,

Masako, and Susie— here with her daughter.

Next I meet Bill Dickerson, at that time the Fukuoka Public Health Officer—

and his interpreter, Dr. Tokuyama.

Unexpectedly, I am sent for temporary duty to Saga,

and live there a month—billeted at the B.O.Q. (Bachelor Officers Qtr.).

One weekend, Bill and I visit Nagasaki—and the Nagasaki Public Health Officer, Capt. Elliot of Cleveland, or rather Brechsville, Ohio,

*obtains a sedan and takes us to the valley
in which the Atom Bomb exploded.*

*First we stop at the partially rebuilt medical school
(what do you think of its chimney?),
then the adjacent ruins of the hospital,*

*with
some
wards
still
standing.*

*I enter the hospital
and wonder about
the patients who
were in here when
the bomb hit.*

*We leave the hospital, pass
a "blasted" tree,*

and go to the hill on which formerly stood the Nagasaki prison (many U.S. P.O.W.s were killed here by the bomb). Elliot takes a picture of the desolate valley,

which you can see behind me.

Then we go to the Catholic church about 1½ miles from the bomb site—where Father Monfetti (you can barely see him in my picture) has assembled some survivors of the bomb.

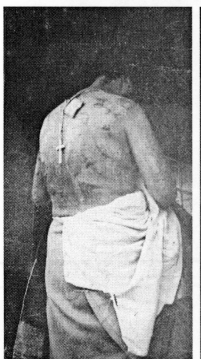

First, a lady shows us the keloids on her back.

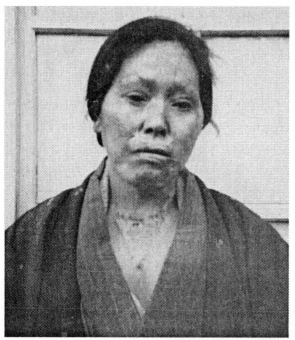

Then, the lady about whom I've already written— she lost six children, had a miscarriage, and suffered severe burns and contractures and keloids.

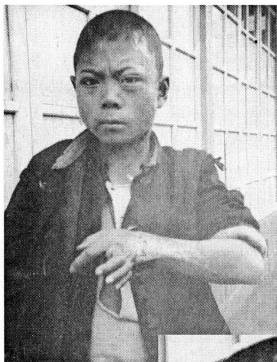

*I've told you
about this poor
boy also.*

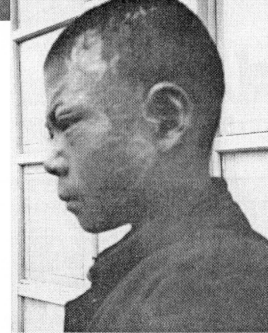

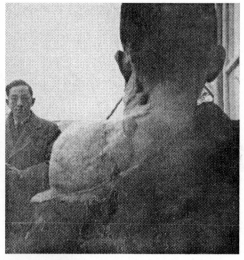

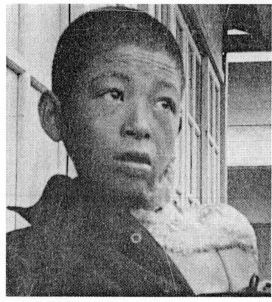

And finally the boy who was swimming when the bomb exploded far in the distance. His eyes ask us "Why?" but he speaks no word. That's all.

The following are five selected photos from pictures taken by my interpreter, Doctor Ichiro Tokuyama:

This landmark marks the site of the atom bomb which exploded about 1000 feet above it. Capt. Eliot, Dr. Tokuyama, Dickerson and I pose—also some boy got into the picture. Tokuyama had a delayed shutter attachment on his camera so that he was able to get into his own picture.

myself and Dickerson

We three were examining this lady when Tokuyama asked us to pose. She was working in a field 1½ miles from the bomb site and suffered "flash burns" on her back after the explosion.

The wall of the Nagasaki prison is behind me.
The prison and many American prisoners of war
were destroyed by the bomb.

The Jap boy was swimming at the time of the explosion and his exposed face, neck and shoulder were burned. He now has a disabling keloid scar. Our smiles may seem incongruous, but the boy was cheerful and we avoided making our examination depressing to him.

I bought the following pictures in a Japanese shop:

The bomb exploded about 1000 ft. in the air, 23,000 people killed, in the rest of the city damage was sporadic, about 60,000 injured, every building suffered some damage, many fires, etc. Someone in the distance was able to photograph the valley at the time.

Father Monfetti, the priest of the church, spent the war in a Jap concentration camp for foreign nationals. He was there when the bomb was dropped—some two years ago— but when he was finally released, he returned to find his church in ruins as you can see.

*This is a school.
Concrete buildings were
not completely destroyed.*

*This is the site of the Nagasaki medical school—about a
half-mile from the bomb site. Only the Junior and Senior
classes were in attendance and they and all the professors
were all killed. The building in the background still
standing was formerly the university hospital.*

REFERENCES

Ackerman, N. W. & Behrens, M. L. (1956). A study of family diagnosis. *American Journal of Orthopsychiatry* 23:26-78.

_____ (1958). *The Psychodynamics of Family Life.* New York: Basic Books.

Bateson, F., Jackson, D., Haley, J. & Weakland, J. (1956). Toward a theory of schizophrenia. *Behavior Science* 1:251-264.

Beels, C. & Ferber, A. (1969). Family therapy: a view. *Family Process* 8:280-318.

Bion, W. R. (1959). *Experiences in Groups.* New York: Basic Books.

Bowen, M. (1957). *Family participation in schizophrenia.* Paper presented at the annual meeting of the American Psychiatric Association, Chicago: May.

_____ (1961). Family psychotherapy. *American Journal of Orthopsychiatry* 31:40-60.

_____ (1965). Family psychotherapy with schizophrenia in the hospital and in private practice. In *Intensive Family Therapy,* ed. Boszormenyi-Nagy and J. Framo, pp. 213-243. New York: Harper and Row.

Buber, M. (1970). *I and Thou.* trans. W. Kaufman {from Buber, M. (1923). *Ich und Du.* Leipzig: Insel-Verlag.}. New York: Charles Scribner and Sons.

Burrow, T. (1927). The group method of analysis. *Psychoanalytic Review* 19:268-280.

Caudill, W. (1958). *The Psychiatric Hospital as a Small Society.* Cambridge: Harvard University Press.

Curry, A. E. (1967). Large therapeutic groups: a critique and appraisal of selected literature. *International Journal of Group Psychotherapy,* October, vol. 17, no. 4.

Edelson, M. (1970). *Sociotherapy and Psychotherapy.* Chicago: University of Chicago Press.

Evans, R. I. (1975). *Carl Rogers; The Man and His Ideas.* New York: E. P. Dutton Paperback.

Ezrial, H. (1950). A psychoanalytic approach to group treatment. *British Journal of Medical Psychiatry* 23:59.

Fairweather, G. W. (1969). *Community Life for the Mentally Ill: An Alternative to Institutional Care.* Chicago: Aldine.

Fierman, E. Y. (2003). Personal communication.

Fierman, L. B., ed. (1965). *Effective Psychotherapy—The Contribution of Hellmuth Kaiser.* New York: Free Press/ Macmillan.

Fierman, L. B., (1965). Myths in the practice of psychotherapy. *Archives of General Psychiatry,* v. 12, April, 408-414.

_____ (1997). *The Therapist Is the Therapy.* Northvale, NJ: Jason Aronson.

Foulkes, S. H. (1964). *Therapeutic Group Analysis.* London: Allen and Unwin.

Framo, J. L. (1975). Personal reflections of a family therapist. *Journal of Marriage and Family Counseling* 1:15-28.

Freud, S. (1921). Group psychology and the analysis of the ego. *Standard Edition* 18:69-143.

Haley, J. (1963). *Strategies of Psychotherapy.* New York: Grune & Stratton.

Haley, J., Alqueurp, B., Labuit, H. A. & Moronge, D. (1974). Multiple family therapy—further developments in changing families. In *A Family Therapy Reader,* pp. 82-95.

Jackson, D. (1958). Family interaction, family homeostasis, and some implications for conjoint family psychotherapy. Paper presented at the meeting of the Academy of Psychoanalysis, New York: May.

Jones, M. (1953). *The Therapeutic Community*. New York: Basic Books.

Kaiser, H. (1962). Emergency. *Psychiatry*, 25:97-118.

____ (1965a). The universal symptom of the psychoneuroses: A search for the conditions of effective psychotherapy. In *Effective Psychotherapy / The Contribution of Hellmuth Kaiser*, ed. L. B. Fierman. New York: Free Press/Macmillan, pp. 14-171.

Kreeger, L. (1975). *The Large Group: Dynamics and Therapy*. London: Constable.

Lewin, K. (1935) *A Dynamic Theory of Personality*. New York: McGraw-Hill.

Lidz, T. (1968). *The Person*. New York: Basic Books.

Lomas, P. (1981). *The Case for a Personal Psychotherapy*. Oxford: Oxford University Press.

____ (1987). *The Limits of Interpretation / What's Wrong With Psychoanalysis*. New York: Penguin Books.

____ (1999). *Doing Good? Psychotherapy Out Of Its Depth*. Oxford: Oxford University Press.

Maslow, A. H. (1956). Self-actualizing People: A Study of Psychological Health. In *The Self: Explorations in Personal Growth*. ed. C. E. Moustakas. New York: Harper & Row, p. 16.

Minear, J. (1979). Evaluation of the weekly community Meeting. Personal communication.

Minuchin, S. (1975). *Families and Family Therapy*. Cambridge: Harvard University Press.

Moreno, J. L. (1946). *Psychodrama*. New York: Beacon House.

____ (1958). *The First Book of Group Psychotherapy*. New York: Beacon House.

Rapoport, R. (1960). *The Community as Doctor*. London: Tavistock.

Reich, W. (1949). *Character Analysis*. New York: Orgone Institute Press.

Rice, A. K. & Turquet, P. M. (1965). *Learning for Leadership: Interpersonal and Intergroup Relations*. London: Tavistock.

Rioch, D. M. (1953). Milieu therapy. *Psychiatry* 16:65-72.

Rogers, C. R. (1942). *Counseling and Psychotherapy*. Boston: Houghton Mifflin

_____ (1951). *Client-Centered Therapy, Its Current Practice, Implications and Theory*. Boston: Houghton Mifflin, pp. 42, 208.

_____ (1961). *On Becoming A Person*. Boston: Houghton Mifflin.

_____ (1977). Learnings in large groups: their implications for the future. La Jolla, CA: Center for Studies of the Person. Private publication.

_____ (1980). *A Way of Being*. Boston: Houghton Mifflin.

Satir, V. (1964). *Conjoint Family Therapy*. Palo Alto, CA: Science and Behavior Books.

Schilder, P. (1938). *Psychotherapy*. New York: Norton.

Slavson, S. R. (1947). *The Practice of Group Therapy*. New York: International Universities Press.

_____ (1956). *The Fields of Group Psychotherapy*. New York: International Universities Press.

Turquet, P. M. (1975). Threats to identity in the large group. In *The Large Group: Dynamics and Therapy*, ed. L. Kreeger. London: Constable.

Von Bertalanffy. (1966). General System Theory and Psychiatry. In *American Handbook of Psychiatry*, vol. 3, ed. S. Arietti, pp. 705-721. New York: Basic Books.

Watzlawick, P., Beaver, J. H. & Jackson, D. D. (1957). *Pragmatics of Human Communication*. New York: Norton and Company.

Whitaker, C. A. (1967). The growing edge in techniques of family therapy. In *Techniques of Family Therapy*. ed. J. Haley and L. Hoffman. New York: Basic Books.

Wolf, A. (1949). The psychoanalysis of groups. *American Journal of Psychiatry* 3:525.

Wynne, L. (1965). Some indications and contraindications for exploring family therapy. In *Intensive Family Therapy*, ed. H. Boszormenyi-Nagy and J. Framo. New York: Harper and Row.

Yalom, I. D. (2002). On Being Helped by Your Patient. In *The Gift of Therapy*. New York: Harper Collins Publishers, pp. 106-108.

INDEX

Louis B. Fierman, M.D., is a graduate of Case Western Reserve University School of Medicine. After completing a rotating internship at Cleveland Metropolitan General Hospital, he entered active duty in the Army and was assigned to Military Government in occupied Japan.

Returning to civilian life in the U.S. in 1949, he entered residency training in internal medicine at Yale, switching to psychiatry with the encouragement of his psychologist wife. He was appointed Chief Resident at both the Yale Psychiatric Institute and the Yale-New Haven Hospital Psychiatric Service, has taught psychotherapy and remains on the clinical faculty of the Yale School of Medicine. He entered psychoanalysis with Hellmuth Kaiser, a psychoanalyst who had broken with traditional and orthodox psychoanalysis to devise a new and more effective psychotherapy. After Kaiser's death, Dr. Fierman published *Effective Psychotherapy*, an anthology of Kaiser's works.

Dr. Fierman has been President of the Connecticut Psychiatric Society, Chief of the Psychiatric Service at the West Haven Veterans Administration Medical Center, Medical Director of Elmcrest Psychiatric Institute and as Medical Director of Psychotherapy Associates, a private practice group in New Haven, Connecticut. He is a Distinguished Life Fellow of the American Psychiatric Association.

Now retired, Dr. Fierman has returned to his childhood interest in classical music and plays the French horn in two local symphony orchestras.

Printed in the United States
54708LVS00001B/133-186